For Girls Only

For Girls Only

Making a Case for Single-Sex Schooling

Janice L. Streitmatter

State University of New York Press

Production by Ruth Fisher
Marketing by Nancy Farrell
Composition by Doric Lay Publishers

Published by
State University of New York Press, Albany

For information, address the State University of New York Press,
State University Plaza, Albany, NY 12246

Library of Congress Cataloging-in-Publication Data
Streitmatter, Janice, 1952–
    For girls only : making a case for single-sex schooling /
Janice L. Streitmatter.
        p. cm.
    Includes bibliographical references (p. 145) and index.
    ISBN 0-7914-4093-1 (hardcover : alk. paper). — ISBN
0-7914-4094-X (pbk. : alk. paper)
    1. Single-sex schools—United States.   2. Women—
Education—United States.   3. Educational equalization—
United States. I. Title.
LB3067.4.S87   1999
372.183'42—dc21   98-26847
                                          CIP

10 9 8 7 6 5 4 3 2 1

Contents

Acknowledgments

This book was possible through the collaborative efforts of many. Priscilla Ross got me started and kept me going. Heather Blair tirelessly collected data for a year. Joanna Marasco collected data for three years, kept the questions fresh, and added invaluable insight into the issues. Bobbie Justice was smart and kind in her editing. Peggy Douglas, the greatest friend possible, kept me steady. The teachers and students who participated in this work were unstinting in their hospitality and generosity.

Thanks to my mother Mary and husband Larry for their particular forms of support. This book is especially for Courtney, who keeps me focused on what is important.

1

On-Site Search

for

Gender Equity

The context of girls-only schooling, particularly in coeducational public schools, became an intriguing one to me almost immediately after I had completed research that examined how teachers committed to gender equity in their teaching practice (Streitmatter 1994). As I observed eight teachers working with students from preschool through high school ages, it became increasingly clear to me that only one of the eight was achieving much in the way of gender equity for her female students. That middle school science teacher believed in the conceptual framework of equity, where she intentionally gave more resources to the girls than the boys. Girls answered her questions and initiated their own, and boys who shouted out answers or in other ways tried to dominate the class were disciplined. She was successful, to some degree, in empowering several of her female students, but she acknowledged that it was a constant struggle, and she sometimes fantasized about having a girls-only class.

At about the same time, a former student, a teacher at a middle school in Arizona, called to say that she was teaching a girls-only math class. She was troubled about the concept, about her capability to do a good job, and about whether the class was even *legal*. She was a strong believer in equality and integration and raised many intriguing questions:

> What possible benefits could be gained by isolating girls, especially in a traditional male domain, such as a math class?

> Didn't girls, alongside boys, have to learn to achieve as well as boys?

> Wouldn't this give boys the idea that girls needed extra help in order to be equal?

While she had read a little about gender issues—and, having two daughters of her own, cared about it—she didn't feel that she had enough preparation in gender equity to adequately cope with these questions. Finally, she asked:

> What about Title IX?

> Wasn't setting up this class illegal, because they were denying boys the ability to enroll?

> How could any of us who were raised with the Civil Rights movement and the women's movement believe that any form of separation could be beneficial?

All good questions. The all-girls class appeared to be antithetical to the values of integration and our hope for a color- and gender-blind society. Was she right in believing that she, and others teaching such a class, need to have a firm foundation in feminist theory and especially pedagogy? Would a teacher in such a class, without that training, do harm? And, of course, she was right about Title IX. When reading the law, it's clear that single-sex classes are stipulated as illegal, except for classes for pregnant girls and one or two other situations.

The contemporary discussion of gender equity, and particularly the experiences of girls in public schools, began with the passage of Title IX in 1972 as part of the Education Amendment Act. The fundamental premises are equal opportunity, equal access, and fully realized integration. Parallel to the principles of racial integration in the broader society, particularly in U.S. public schools, Title IX focuses on providing full access to participation in all functions of schooling, regardless of gender. In other words, with only minimal exceptions, discrimination based on gender in public schools is prohibited.

Through the 1970s and 1980s, female and male students found the barriers were lowered to auto mechanics and home economics classes as well as interscholastic sports. Most of the prestigious universities and colleges that previously had admitted only men began to enroll women as undergraduates. The outer layer of discrimination, denial of access, was peeled away. Female, as well as male, students found greater freedom of choice and participation within the realm of public schooling, as enforced by public policy.

And now, as the next century looms, the question is not whether Title IX has provided support for gains in gender equity, particularly for female students. Rather, it is whether by virtue of the rigid way in which it is interpreted, Title IX allows us to go further in fulfilling the original intent of true equality.

In Section 106.35, Title IX addresses single-sex schools and classrooms:

> [A] recipient [of federal funds] which is a local education agency (LEA) shall not, on the basis of sex, exclude any person from admission to (a) any institution of vocational education operated by such recipient; or (b) any other school educational unit operated by such recipient, unless such recipient otherwise makes available to such person, pursuant to the same policies and criteria of admission, courses, services, and facilities comparable to each course, service, and facility offered in or through such schools. (Hollinger 1993)

Because Title IX does not explicitly regulate admission policies in K–12 public schools, except for vocational schools, single-sex schools are not prohibited when comparable educational opportunities are made available to the other gender in a comparable facility. The key word is *comparable*.

Recent U.S. Supreme Court decisions regarding admission of female cadets to The Military Citadel of South Carolina (The Citadel) (Sanchez 1996) and Virginia Military Institute (VMI) (Excerpts . . . 1996) demonstrate the Court's current interpretation of *comparable* as *separate but equal*. The Court ruled, in both cases, that there was no demonstrable reason for the denial of admission of women to these military institutions.

In the case of VMI, a leadership training program for women was established at nearby Mary Baldwin College. The plaintiff convinced the Court that neither the curriculum, the methods of instruction, nor the facility at Mary Baldwin were similar enough to VMI to be considered comparable.

The fundamental argument by The Citadel in defending male-only admission was that there was a need for a single-sex school for military leadership training, and in admitting women, the culture of the program would be fundamentally altered, rendering the school unable to fulfill its mission. Here too the Court supported the principles of integration and equal access by determining admissions policies of The Citadel to be discriminatory, based on gender.

Courts have held similar views on single-sex, single-race public schools. During the late 1980s and early 1990s, school districts in Baltimore, Milwaukee, and New York opened African American, publicly funded academies for males with the intent of providing unique schools for African American males. The establishment of these schools was predicated on evidence that African American males in many urban neighborhoods are at greater risk for dropping out of school, for delinquent or criminal behavior, for lower career aspirations, and for early violent death than African American girls.

The curriculum was purposely chosen to reflect positively on African American male contributions and experiences, and the schools were largely staffed by African American men. In all cases, the schools' boards or the courts ruled that these academies had to admit girls or close, because they violated Title IX by not providing comparable settings for girls. Although public policy allows for the existence of single-sex schools, in practice, there are very few that go unchallenged, regardless of the case made for purpose and need.

Despite the federal prohibition of establishing single-sex classes, a growing number of local schools' education practitioners have turned to the creation of girls-only classes in order to address issues of gender bias. However, Section 106.34 of Title IX specifically states (with extremely limited exceptions) that single-sex classrooms within coeducational K–12 schools are not allowed:

> A recipient shall not provide any course or otherwise carry out any of its education program or activity separately on the basis of sex. . . .

The three exceptions to this regulation are contact sports, classes where human sexuality is taught, and classes for pregnant girls, all based on an argument of the need for safety or privacy (Hollinger 1993). With those few exceptions, the development of girls-only classes is clearly a violation of public policy.

Beginning of the Study

After receiving the call from the middle school teacher and pondering the questions about her girls-only class, two doctoral students and I observed the class, as well as other classes at her school and those at two high schools. During a four-year period, we interviewed teachers and others, talked with school administrators, chatted with a number of parents, and spent many hours interviewing the girls while they were enrolled in the classes and, in some cases, for several years after that.

I also spent some time at a well-established, private girls' academy in Connecticut in order to talk with administrators, teachers, and students who were connected with that school, the existence of which was based in part on the fact that it is single-sex. Would people within these vastly disparate sites talk about the same issues with regard to single-sex schooling for girls? Over time, it became apparent to me that a girls-only environment has value, whether the girls are from upper- and upper-middle-class homes in Connecticut or they are middle class or poor and living in the western United States. I became convinced that single-sex public schools and/or single-sex classes in coeducational public schools should be an available option, especially for girls who do not have the economic means to choose private, single-sex schools. While the comments of the interviewed adults connected with the girls-only classes in the public schools were convincing, the voices of the students who participated in the classes were compelling.

Self-Esteem and Safety

Other factors, especially declining self-esteem (beginning in early adolescence) and safety, increasingly impressed me as critical issues that deserved consideration. While I addressed the self-esteem issue through conversations with the girls and teachers, the safety issue was not examined directly. But it became clear that many of the girls valued their girls-only experiences in part because they felt better about themselves, and, in some sense, safer.

Although the qualitative data in this book do not present as vivid a picture of declining self-esteem in girls as that in Pipher's *Reviving Ophelia* (1994), some of the issues are the same. Pipher's work illustrates the dramatic downward spiral of self-esteem and confidence in early-adolescent and adolescent girls. Pipher's accounts of the struggle of girls moving from childhood through the mine field of adolescence to adulthood examine issues of eating disorders, coping with mixed messages about what and who to be, as well as issues that have direct bearing on schooling.

As girls' holistic views of themselves change for the worse during these years, girls also appear to reconstruct their views of themselves in relation to particular subject matter taught in schools. Pipher speaks of one girl after another who, in junior high or middle school, describes herself as no longer liking math, no longer being smart in math, and feeling uncomfortable or afraid in science classes. Many of the girls in her work also have learned to "dummy down." That is a lesson we would not expect with the advances women are making regarding greater opportunities in the work place and the *politically correct* rhetoric that *women can do anything men can.*

Pipher found, and our study suggests, that young adolescent and adolescent girls of today sometimes experience peer pressure—from boys and other girls—to avoid getting good grades. Smart girls in elementary school get good grades, but smart girls in middle and high school do so at the risk of being unpopular, snubbed, and called names. Pipher's 1994 book depicts the extent to which so many young women are at risk in our schools; the risks are physical through sexual harassment and assault, academic through declining confidence and self-esteem, and emotional as they struggle to define themselves.

In *SchoolGirls* [sic](1994), Orenstein also describes the phenomenon of the decline of self-esteem in young adolescent girls. Conversations with, and observations of, girls of diverse socioeconomic and ethnic backgrounds from two California middle schools reveal the girls' sense that they are less visible in classes, that they are less often heard. They mean this literally, in the sense that they are called on in the classroom less often than boys, and metaphorically in that their capabilities are taken less seriously than those of boys by teachers, boys, and other girls.

Sexual Harassment

Some of the girls in Orenstein's work also felt victimized by sexual harassment in the schools and in their neighborhoods. One story is of Jeanie, who was taunted by boys about the size of her breasts. The principal was frustrated by Jeanie's lack of assertion in defending herself and in seeking help from the adults in the school. The principal also was frustrated by the silence and acquiescence of the other girls. This prompts the question: Do girls take it as a matter of course that they will be called names, restrained, and physically accosted by boys?

Lee, Croninger, Linn, and Chen (1996) examined the extent to which middle and high school students reported that they had been sexually harassed or that they had perpetrated harassment on someone else. Their results indicated that vast numbers of students believe they are victims of sexual harassment (83 percent of the girls and 60 percent of the boys in a sample of 1,203 students) and that girls are much more likely to be the recipients of it. Their work also reviews a number of theories about why sexual harassment exists. These theories range from the biological theory that says due to hormones and greater body size, males can be expected to be the perpetrators of sexual harassment, to the critical theory approach that stipulates sexual harassment occurs because within the broader society, sexual aggression is tolerated and even encouraged through the media and Madison Avenue advertising, as an instrument of capitalism.

Lee et al. (1996) call for schools to become places that are sensitive and open to discussions of values that might lead to greater understanding of issues, such as sexual harassment, and thereby have the effect of diminishing it. If taken seriously, this constitutes a call for considerable reconstruction of schools. According to most feminist theories (e.g., Belenky, Clinchy, Goldberg, and Tarule 1986; Lewis 1990; Stone 1994), schools are places where power resides with males and indeed the entire structure is male dominated. In order to create schools where gender bias no longer exists, where females can be equal participants and beneficiaries of a positive educational experience, the existing framework of schools would have to be de-constructed and redesigned to become very different places. This process would have to go far beyond an emphasis on value of the individual, where issues of gender could be topics of discussion.

There is no question that school administrators, teachers, and parents today are more alert to issues of sexual harassment in schools than in earlier years. Most schools are now required to have written policies about sexual harassment along with defined punishments for it. But policies and consequences only work if harassment is understood for what it is, and then reported.

In 1989, our daughter, in the first grade, happened to mention that she could not wear a skirt to school the following day, because the boys had declared it "flip-up day." At the time, she did not know to call this incident *harassment,* but she certainly knew something was wrong. She also understood that this group of boys should not have that kind of power over her. Further, she decided that if the adults in the school could not or would not protect the other girls and her from this aggression, she would forgo wearing skirts altogether.

By the time she was in sixth grade, she had experienced another incident. Almost daily, her writing teacher left the classroom to supervise another group of students in an adjacent conference room. When the teacher was out of the room, several boys would circle the tables where eight girls were seated, and through motions and sounds, simulate sexual intercourse. The girls experienced this on an almost daily basis for four months before several of us parents learned about it.

"What did you do?" we asked our daughter.

"We tried to ignore them," she said.

We were stunned, just as the principal in Orenstein's (1994) story was exasperated by the girls' silence. How many other occasions had there been in which she and the other girls accepted harassment and looked the other way? How often, and with good reason, had they believed that the adults in the school would not take their concerns seriously? In this case, the boys were disciplined by receiving a lecture about appropriate classroom behavior, and the teacher was directed not to leave the classroom. The incident was explained as a lapse in discipline, when perhaps it should have been seen as a great deal more.

In *SchoolGirls,* Orenstein (1994) tells of other times of sexual harassment that the girls she interviewed had experienced. Most were not reported, and the girls tended to internalize them as part of their expected experience, hurtful as it was.

Although sexual harassment is not directly addressed in our four-year study of girls-only schooling, the issues of self-esteem and safety were examined in various ways, and I was increasingly convinced that the girls-only environment provided the students with a place of respite. They seemed to create their own culture in which they did not need to struggle with issues of classroom control by boys. They knew they were visible and heard and that they could focus and participate. The girls convinced me that their girls-only classes were right for them, regardless of the theoretical drawbacks to segregation as well as the more concrete problem of violation of Title IX.

Obviously, my intent in this book is to make a case for girls-only classes in public, coeducational schools. In the following chapter, we will examine current public policy, specifically Title IX, in the face of contradicting local practice. Folded into the debate are the positions of the National Organization for Women on single-sex schooling, the function of a division of the U.S. Department of Education in hearing complaints about violations of Title IX, and the views of administrators who have been, or currently are, involved in girls-only settings. Later we will briefly examine the history of females' schooling in the United States, current research on the state of gender equity for girls in coeducational public school, and a review of feminist theory. Interviews with teachers, administrators, and more importantly students, provide supportive data that strengthen the case for girls-only classes in public schools. Results of this longitudinal, qualitative study will suggest that we revisit the intent and current limitations of Title IX.

It should be noted at this time that fictitious names for the profiled schools, as well as the teachers and students who actively participated in this study, have been substituted for their real names.

2

$\mathcal{P}$ublic $\mathcal{P}$olicy

versus

$\mathcal{L}$ocal $\mathcal{P}$ractice

P re-twentieth-century educational institutions tended to
point out differences in the two genders. In contrast,
the intent of both feminists and public policy in the
early stages of the contemporary women's movement, beginning in the 1960s, was to disavow any fundamental differences
between the sexes. In order to succeed in pressing for full participation of girls and women in arenas formerly male dominated, the case had to be made that females were the full
equal of males, that is, they had to be viewed as the same.
Only if women were to be viewed the same as men could they
expect to receive the same rights and opportunities as men.

To acknowledge difference is to run the risk of devaluing
any female who is different from those of the valued male-gen-
der class. When we begin to ask the question, "What might be
different about girls than boys?" it too easily becomes restated
as "What's wrong with girls?" It is difficult for many of us to
make the statement that we believe females are different from
males in ways other than the obvious physical ones. Whether
we believe that the differences stem from socialization practices or are of a more inherent nature has some importance,
but perhaps when we are considering how to best help girls in

schools, it is not the critical question. Feminist and critical theorists suggest that the oppressive nature of girls' experiences in school is systemic and inextricably tied to the broader culture. In order for girls' experiences to be recast, schools would have to be dramatically reordered, constituting nearly revolutionary shifts in what and whom we value. This shift would have to be reflected in all aspects of the culture. Perhaps this will occur, but it doesn't appear imminent.

In the meantime, girls continue to experience declining levels of self-esteem during adolescence, sexual harassment in the hallways and classrooms, and alienation in science and math classrooms. Whether girls are different from boys because we adults interact differently with them, whether because of biological influences, or a combination of the two, it is difficult to ignore the fact that, as a rule, girls and boys act, talk, and feel differently, and female students in our coeducational schools tend not to grow academically or emotionally as the male students grow.

The fact that girls struggle with issues that boys do not, especially during early adolescence and adolescence, has not escaped the notice of most educators. From the level of policy maker to practitioner, attempts are made in most schools to address gender-equity issues. However, the framework for addressing these issues is nearly always that of equality and relies on the premise that there are no differences between girls and boys. Through opportunities of equal access and equal participation in classrooms, it is assumed that outcomes will be equal without regard to gender and that, while individual boys and girls will achieve at various levels, neither gender group will be identifiable as more successful. Though the initial openings that Title IX has created are important, we are confronted with abundant evidence that suggests this simply has not been enough.

The current construction of coeducational classrooms can be problematic for girls in a number of ways. Two alternative environments exist: all-girls schools and all-girls classrooms, neither of which is new. As chronicled in the next chapter, girls' academies have existed in the United States for nearly two centuries. Now, as in the past, these academies offer upper- and upper-middle-class girls an education that prepares them to take their places in the highest levels of social and occupational standing that society at any one time has allowed. In earlier times, young women graduates moved on to high-status social roles, but today the young women coming from these schools do that as well as attain high occupational status.

Single-sex classes in coeducational schools are not a new construction either. In earlier days of coeducational public schooling, due to differentiated curricula for girls and boys, many classes either were explicitly or implicitly for one gender or the other. Explicit gender segregation was found in home economics and shop classes, while the more subtle gender separation was found in academic areas such as math and science. These were the classes that girls often were advised to avoid.

Recently, geographically isolated progress has been made in establishing single-sex classes, and public school educators are increasingly targeting math and science as the classes that might be important to construct as girls-only environments in middle and high schools. The development of these classes is in direct response to gender equity concerns, particularly issues of academic achievement and self-esteem.

Classes for African American males as well as single-sex classes in math and science for girls in public coeducational schools have generated discussion about the efficacy of creating separate and unique places for these groups of students to be taught and to learn. Nearly always, the rationale for these separate classes, programs, or schools is that a specific group of students will benefit from the experience of being together without having to compete for resources with other students.

Tensions associated with these single-sex settings appear to be related to the interpretation of public policy, Title IX, tied in with the more philosophical debate of whether any form of separation is profitable to an isolated group, regardless of the soundness of the arguments for the creation of the class.

Public Education: Issues Involving Single-Gender Schools and Programs, published in May 1996 (U.S. General Accounting Office), summarizes many of the issues surrounding single-sex settings in the public sector. The synopsis of the rationale in support of the organization of single-sex settings examines briefly the research of Riordan (1990), Bailey (1992), and Sadker and Sadker (1995), which suggests that settings in which students are separated by gender are beneficial with regard to academic achievement and self-esteem. The portion of the document that provides the counter argument is devoted to a discussion of public policy, that is, both Title IX as well as the 14th Amendment to the Constitution. Several court cases concerning gender discrimination have been heard within the context of this amendment, which relates to equal protection. Although in a number of cases single-sex settings have been ruled illegal, the GAO report does not review or cite any research that suggests single-sex settings are injurious to any group.

Vorchheimer v. School District of Philadelphia (1976) was brought about by girls who were seeking admission to Central High School in Philadelphia. This school, which admitted only boys, was one of two single-gender public high schools in the city. The court originally ruled that because a comparable high school existed for girls, the girls did not have a sufficient case. However, the following year, girls again brought suit, contending that Central High was a substantially different and better facility, and Girls High was not comparable. In this case, the court agreed, requiring the school to develop admission standards that were not based in part on gender. Girls High, however, remains single-sex.

In another gender-discrimination case, *Mississippi University for Women v. Hogan* (1982), the court took the case of a man, Hogan, who sued the University when he was denied admission because he was male. The five to four decision was in favor of Hogan, with the court's majority saying that "a state needs to show an 'exceedingly persuasive justification' for classifying individuals on the basis of gender" (U.S. General Accounting Office 1996, 12).

Most recently, the federal Supreme Court heard the gender-discrimination cases against Virginia Military Institute (VMI) and The Citadel. In the former, a women's leadership institute was established at nearby Mary Baldwin College, which was intended to represent a comparable experience to that of The Citadel. The Court determined that the Mary Baldwin program was not substantially the same as that of VMI and ruled that VMI could not base admissions on gender. Shortly after that ruling, the Court ruled that the desire of The Citadel to maintain their male culture was not sufficient reason to restrict their admissions to men only.

No case recently has been heard regarding single-sex elementary or secondary schools, programs, or classes, although some educators connected with these settings express some wariness about impending complaints. As of spring 1997, only a few complaints had been filed, according to Doreen Dennis (personal communication, 15 October 1996) of the Department of Education, Title IX division. Dennis said that generally, when complaints are filed:

> We try to work things out voluntarily. Pretend we did find a violation of Title IX. We give the school district an opportunity to change whatever was in violation. That is what happens in the great majority of cases. Usually if the school district hears about a complaint, they want to make a change. There isn't even a hearing. We give them the opportunity to fix it. If they don't, there are two different ways we might go. One is to go into an administrative hearing in which we would try to terminate the federal financial assistance. In the other, we refer the case to the justice department, and have them take it to court. (D. Dennis 1997)

When asked if it is rare for a school district to refuse to change the single-sex structure under complaint, Dennis said it is very unusual. She indicated that the current interpretation of Title IX has remained consistent with the initial intent of the mandate. Any publicly funded schooling institution that is found to be discriminating, based on gender, risks losing federal assistance. Further, the current legal climate, reflected by the recent Supreme Court decisions in the cases of The Citadel and VMI, appears to be reinforcing the conceptual framework within which Title IX is interpreted. Any class, program, or school that is constructed outside of the framework of equal distribution of resources for all is considered to be deviating from the intent of the law.

When asked how research findings in the area of single-sex groupings have affected the interpretation of Title IX, Dennis suggested that there was little impact.

> I'm glad that you're working on the research end of it. It just seems like the research makes suggestions but . . . I think, needless to say, we're going to be guided by the court interpretations and our own regulations. (D. Dennis 1997)

Dennis's comments seem to reflect the conflict between the intent of public policy and the direction of local practice in the cases of the establishment of single-sex settings.

Rationale for Single-Sex Classes

Beginning in the early 1990s, several school districts located in large, urban areas attempted to create classes for African American male students. The decision was based on the demographic as well as other data indicating that this group of young people was particularly at risk. The belief was that an important intervention might be the creation of a class where both the curriculum and the pedagogy would be constructed to address issues of African American male students only. For example, curriculum would highlight the contributions of African American males, and as many of the teachers as possible would be African American men. Girls were not invited to be part of these classes, and almost immediately Title IX was invoked by individuals or groups who believed that while the creation of these single-sex/single-race settings might be beneficial to African American males, they violated the civil rights of female students.

During the fall of 1996, telephone conversations were held with individuals affiliated with several schools, where, at one time, an attempt had been made to create an environment for African American male students only. At Malcolm X Middle School in Milwaukee, Wisconsin, the principal, Kenneth Holt, reported:

The original intent here was to have it all boys. We ran into the National Organization for Women [NOW], who turned to a lawsuit back four or five years ago. So we had to make sure that we—and also the Title IX issue—we had to make sure that we were not discouraging young ladies from being here. What we do is have a lot of things at school on the weekends that are single-sex.

Another thing, at that time we had settled within the process of trying to redo the deseg agreement, and the Board made it clear we absolutely were not going to get into a legal battle again.

Now we have Afro-centric curriculum modules that we use, that we integrate along with the regular standards in terms of expectations or the curriculum. We infuse it on a daily basis. For example, on Tuesday, Thursday and sometimes on the weekend, we have the rites of passage for young men. We have many mentors who come in and talk to boys in single-sex environments. Just like we have Black Women's Network, a professional women's organization working with girls on Saturdays, once a week. (K. Holt, personal communication, 23 October 1996)

The Martin Luther King Elementary School also was designated originally as a site for focus on African American male students. In the fall of 1996, the principal there, Josephine Mosley, described her school's situation in much the same way as the principal at Malcolm X:

The Board wouldn't agree, so here we're coeducational. The intent was to raise the achievement of African American males, but in order to do that it didn't necessarily mean they had to be by themselves. As far as I know, there are no single-sex classes anywhere in the district. (J. Mosley, personal communication, 23 October 1996)

At the same time, in the case of the existence of girls-only classes without the emphasis on race, inquiries were made at several levels. Carol Rezba, the math specialist at the State Department of Education in Virginia, had some vague knowledge of girls-only classes, especially in math, but was certain that there weren't any in her jurisdiction:

> I know one school division called me last year and they were thinking about implementing it, and it's a hot topic because there are groups opposed to it. Because of that, the state will not set policy for that. They are asking their own school boards to make a policy decision with their lawyers fully aware of what they're doing. As a state worker I have to tell them that the state will not make a decision for them. They have to make it at the local level and be locally accountable for it.
>
> I think there are people out there who are doing these classes, being quiet about it. You get a lot more implemented when you don't open your mouth. (C. Rezba, personal communication, 22 October 1996)

Dr. Geraldine Myles, principal of Girls High School in Philadelphia spoke about the makeup of Girls High as well as its success (personal communication, 16 October 1996). She said:

> This is a school for academically talented public school girls and we send about 98% off to college. We have an average daily attendance of over 95% each day and 300–400 honor roll students. So, in spite of the fact that we have almost 50% below the poverty level and over 50% of ethnic backgrounds other than white, we do quite well. The school is moving toward its 150th year.
>
> My fear is that we won't stay open. There are arguments for and against everything, and I think that this is not a school for everybody, but we do not discriminate, and we provide a college preparatory program, and the girls meet our expectations. We teach over 16 college-level courses. And we're enrolled with students from 10th through 12th grade. We're dealing with a different time from when the school was formed. Then that was the general way things were done. The reasons for the school's existence is different now than then. Recent information

says that girls benefit from this kind of setting. Sometimes I don't know how you can go with it in today's world. But here we think we are providing important opportunities and we are going to try to continue to do so. (G. Myles 1996)

The interviews with these officials in public schools (not among the schools observed in this study) reflect conflict between policy and practice. In the initial cases, interest in— and attempts to design—learning environments of single-sex/single-race were abandoned not because the educators involved determined that the creation of these settings would be detrimental to the students for whom they were to serve, nor to the students who would not participate. Rather they were abandoned because of the potential threat of litigation, based on Title IX.

The interview with Dr. Myles suggests that despite the 150 years of history and tradition of Girls High, there is concern that, due to the current political context, separation under any circumstances is detrimental and illegal and the school may encounter discrimination action based on Title IX.

Young Women's Leadership Academy

The debate about another school, East Harlem Young Women's Leadership Academy, may embody many of the issues surrounding the separation of young women from a coeducational learning environment within the public school domain. The academy opened its doors in fall 1996, as a girls-only public school within the New York City public school system. Both Rudy Crew, Chancellor, and Janet Rizzo, Deputy Chancellor for Curriculum, decided not to prohibit the opening of the school, in spite of vocal opposition from the New York Civil Liberties Union, the New York chapter of the National Organization for Women, and a local statute from 1991 that prohibits single-sex public schools (Tabor, July 22, 1996).

Identifying itself as a program rather than a school, the Leadership Academy may be considered a structure parallel to other programs that exist within the city's twenty-seven-year-old desegregation law. Over the years, a number of alternative programs have been instituted under this provision without needing the consent of the Chancellor's office (Steinberg, 14 August 1996).

The initial concept for the program began with the Center for Educational Innovation, part of the Manhattan Institute. The center is funded through an endowment from Andrew and Ann Rubenstein Tisch, based on the premise that ". . . girls, particularly in poor neighborhoods like East Harlem, perform better when boys are not in the classroom" (Steinberg, July 16, 1996). The program, although funded through the normal means by which other schools within the New York public school system are funded, also is subsidized, at least in part, by private funds from the Center for Educational Innovation.

Unlike Girls High in Philadelphia and Western High in Baltimore, the other longstanding girls-only public high school in the country, the promotional literature about the Leadership Academy, as well as the initial admissions process, appears to quite explicitly exclude boys. As the entering class of 55 seventh graders was being formed, school officials indicated that "even if a boy did apply, they [were] not sure whether they would accept him, considering that the interview process is geared toward finding young girls interested in learning to be leaders" (Steinberg, 16 July 1996).

Initial negative reaction to the formation of a girls-only program or school in East Harlem might be encapsulated by remarks from Norman Siegel, the executive director of the New York Civil Liberties Union: "If they are not going to do any affirmative outreach to boys then that is not acceptable" (Steinberg, July 16, 1996).

As the 1996–97 school year progressed, the debate continued. Ann Conners, President of the New York City chapter of the National Organization for Women (NOW) and Seymour Fliegel of the Manhattan Institute had met at New York University (NYU) in a debate about the Young Women's Leadership Academy. In a public statement (copied by Conners to the author of this study by fax on 17 January 1997), Conners described the stance of NOW in ways similar to those she presented in the NYU debate, making it clear that NOW stands squarely in opposition to the creation of any schools or classes that are designed for the purpose of separating one group of students from the rest of the population. Conners (1997) believes that in supporting a single-sex school, such as the East Harlem Young Women's Leadership Academy, irreparable harm will be done to the longstanding fight for equalization of women into all aspects of society:

> We are told that this [Young Women's Leadership Academy] is a good thing. But this is an illusion. Creating this separate *public* school violates city, state, and federal anti-discrimination law. It also flies in the face of public education's mandate to develop a literate population able to transcend historical barriers based on race and gender in society and in the work force. It does not teach or promote tolerance, multiculturalism or sex equity in schools or in society. (Conners 1997)

Conners suggests, on behalf of NOW, that the creation of a girls-only school is a "band-aid" approach, and that by virtue of its existence, the school harms not only those girls attending, but women in general. Isolation of females is a dangerous action that further perpetuates a separate but unequal climate. Conners lists a number of remedies for gender inequity, all of which she believes can be realized within the context of public, coeducational institutions:

- Already-existing programs on sex equity in public schools be implemented and enforced.

- Parents are educated and organize to fight for strict enforcement of equal opportunity mandates for student access to quality public education.

- City, state, and federal funding are increased for technical assistance to schools to implement race and gender fair policies and practices in public education.

- In-service training for teachers and administrators is increased, with sessions centering on implementing equitable practices in the classroom.

- A bias-free curriculum is used which accurately reflects the achievements of women and people of color in our society.

- Affirmative action is implemented at all levels of the school system. This will provide critical role models needed by all students.

- Action is taken to increase funding for girls' sports. (Conners 1997)

The other side of the debate is provided by proponents of girls-only settings. In a telephone conversation in January 1997, after the NYU debate, Seymour Fliegel, the Senior Fellow at the Center for Educational Innovation of the Manhattan Institute, described the Institute's reason for supporting the creation of the East Harlem Young Women's Leadership Academy:

> The whole rationale went something like this: Young women up until around the seventh grade seem to do OK in elementary school. Most probably, sometimes they do better than boys in math. But beginning around seventh grade, their own expectations begin to change and the culture of the school gives them a message that basically says, "Don't show you're too smart, too aggressive," whatever you want to call it. They take on those characteristics. There's enough research around that says this affects all girls. [At this school] a girl is president of the class, the best actress/actor, the best athlete. That should show something to other students, that it's OK to do the best you can. That's what the school is really about. And it's about leadership because as a result of those attitudes of lowering expectations, taking a back seat, you diminish your possibilities for leadership. And math and science was just an area that we wanted to make certain [was emphasized] since those are areas that young women don't enter into. (S. Fliegel, personal communication, January 17, 1997)

When asked to remark about the opposition to the Leadership Academy, Fliegel said:

They [NOW and the Civil Liberties Union] have legal opposition. We [Manhattan Institute and the Leadership Academy] have educational reasons for doing it. (Fliegel 1997)

This last statement appears to encapsulate the debate in New York and elsewhere. Organizations or individuals opposing the development of single-sex settings, especially those that are publicly funded, look to public policy for support of their views. Title IX, according to current interpretation, argues against any form of group isolation within the public sector.

However, as Fliegel has pointed out, local practice, in the case of the Young Women's Leadership Academy, as well as in other places in the United States, points to the research that clearly indicates gender-inequitable practice and outcomes in public, coeducational schools.

In chapter 6, we will show how practitioners, the teachers interviewed in this study, have turned to girls-only settings in order to address issues connected with girls and schooling. While many believe in the intent of Title IX, they practice their teaching in schools where this intent is not realized, nor is it likely to be. Further, the girls they teach in these settings have convinced them that they are doing the right thing, regardless of the strictures of federal public policy.

But first, let's examine in chapter 3 a brief history of girls' schooling.

3

A Brief History
of
Girls-Only Schooling

Separate schooling for females is not a new concept. It is reasonable to say that some form of girls-only schooling has been present for centuries. For example, during the late Renaissance, female academies emerged in Europe providing curricula that emphasized *women's arts*. Today, single-sex schooling for girls and women is present in the form of single-sex preparatory schools and to a much lesser extent as single-sex classes in coeducational public schools. The original consequence of single-sex schooling was that of isolation, social reproduction, and oppression of women, while the current goal is to provide females with learning environments that provide every opportunity for future success in a competitive and heterogeneous world.

This chapter provides a brief overview of historical trends that have helped shape the educational milieu for female students in the United States today. Early educational structures and curricula tended to be based on the assumption that women were different and less than men. When schooled, girls and women were given basic lessons in literacy as well as in how to assume their socially appropriate roles. These roles nearly always were private and without power.

Men worked in the public world, owned property, and made decisions. Women tended to work in private or closed spheres. When earning wages in positions of absolute powerlessness, their decisions were of domestic not public consequence, and they had no legal rights. Only a minuscule number of women experienced education that prepared them for other than these situations.

Early Education of Women

Late in the sixth century, there was a brief period in Western Europe when a small number of women were educated with men in monasteries. However, it was not until the Protestant Reformation in the fifteenth century that education for females was seriously considered. Martin Luther advocated the teaching of reading to females as well as males, so that they could read and understand the Bible (suddenly available to large numbers of people, thanks to invention of the printing press). Far from being a social reconstructionist, Luther was interested in educating all classes and both genders in order to spread the new Protestantism.

While Luther and John Calvin argued about religious dogma, they agreed on the importance of educating across social and gender groups. Calvinist Protestantism arrived in New England with the Puritans, and with it the belief that girls too should learn to read. Although larger numbers of females had access to the basics of schooling than in earlier times, it would be inaccurate to assume that girls' educational opportunities were equal to that of boys. Even those who attended school the same amount of time as boys experienced a curriculum that was less academically oriented. Girls nearly always received a lower level of education (Clabaugh and Razycki 1990).

During the late Renaissance, female academies in Europe provided girls from the upper classes a curriculum that emphasized such subjects as sewing and household management, so they might fulfill their predetermined roles as wives and mothers. Girls from the lower social classes learned skills from other women in their families and their communities that were commensurate with their social class and prescribed social role.

By the end of the eighteenth century, *dame schools* (so called because young women were often the teachers) had been established in New England; however, other parts of the new country had very few schools open to middle- and lower-class children. Dame schools were created to provide the basics in reading, writing, and arithmetic and were open to boys and girls who attended from the ages of about seven through ten. The curriculum differed by gender, however, as did the amount of time spent receiving the education. Curricula for girls included mandatory lessons in needlework, which had the effect of lessening the amount of time given to the academic subjects. Further, girls were less likely to attend at all, given the longstanding belief that academic skills were less necessary for girls than boys. When allowed by their families to attend school at all, girls attended less often and left school earlier than boys (Stock 1978).

In the early nineteenth century, a campaign to increase girls' access to secondary education in the United States was started by women such as Hannah Mather Crocker, who wrote *Observations on the Real Rights of Women,* and Emma Willard, who wrote, among other things, *Plan for Improving Female Education* (Stock 1978). Crocker's primary concern was to expand girls' postprimary educational opportunities, while Willard worked toward ways of increasing the quality of pedagogy and standards in girls' education. Willard was particularly concerned about girls having the opportunity to study subjects that were considered the domain of boys. On her own, she studied all areas of math and geography and then taught what she knew to other women, who in turn would teach these subjects to their female students. Through her efforts, the Troy Female Seminary (now Emma Willard School) opened in 1821 in Troy, New York, with a curriculum that included math and science.

Other women also were instrumental in expanding opportunities for women's education. In the western regions of the United States, Catherine Beecher helped to create normal schools, which were organized around a curriculum of domestic science, or training to become a good housewife. Mary Lyon founded Mount Holyoke Female Seminary in 1837. This school differed from its predecessors in that the three years' course work more closely replicated that of men's private secondary academies. English, mathematics, sciences, religion, fine arts, French, and gymnastics were required. Domestic arts was not included in the curriculum.

The early nineteenth century also saw the beginning of secondary public school education for females. The first girls' high school was opened in Worcester, Massachusetts, in 1824, followed by the New York Female High School in 1826. Where girls' high schools did exist, the purpose of the schools was made clear. The curriculum was intended to provide women with an education that would enable them to become fit wives for educated men. These schools, however, were the exception to the rule. Generally, because most communities had no compulsory attendance laws, nor laws that called for publicly funded schools, girls simply were not admitted to schools.

Following the Civil War, not only did the number of secondary schools increase sharply, expanding from cities to rural areas, but the attendance demographics changed as well. By 1890, more students were enrolled in public than private schools, and despite the fact that most schools offered college preparatory curricula that really were not intended for girls, girls outnumbered boys in attendance. Schools had become places where middle-class girls bided time before marriage, while lower- and middle-class boys often left to start work, thereby explaining the predominance of girls in public high schools.

It was toward the end of the nineteenth century that, despite the adherence of most educators to the enduring notion that women's educational needs and abilities were quite different from men's, coeducational secondary schools became more prevalent than single-sex private or public schools (Tyack and Hansot 1990). The first coeducational colleges were Oberlin (1833) and Antioch (1853). It is interesting to note that Oberlin's reason for accepting women was in order to help the male students with regard to their views of women. Women were admitted so that men might gain a more "wholesome and realistic view of women" (Stock 1978, 190) than they would if educated in an all-male environment. While these women students probably benefited from the higher education, any successful experiences they might have had cannot be credited to these colleges' considering their educational needs. Instead, the women's presence could be considered part of the curriculum for the male students, something along the lines of *Introduction to Females, Sociology 101.*

As the nineteenth century advanced, some of the state universities, including those in Maine, Michigan, Wisconsin, and Iowa, began to admit women to their degree programs; however, the exclusive universities and colleges in the Northeast did not follow this trend. As a result, women's colleges were established, such as Vassar (1860), Wellesley (1875), Smith (1875), and Bryn Mawr (1880). Although Smith developed entrance standards and a curriculum comparable to those in exclusive men's colleges, many of the women's colleges chose to modify the curriculum to one that was believed to better represent women's higher education needs. For example, rather than teaching traditional chemistry, Vassar taught culinary chemistry and toxicology.

The Twentieth Century

During this century, educational opportunities for women have, on the face of it, been transformed from marginal to mainstream. Along with equal legal rights, women have equal access to schools and the curricula within them; however, as the extent of women's opportunities has changed, the basic culture of schools has not. The Euro-male centric nature of schools remains largely intact, and those who participate in U.S. schools are required to acclimate to that culture if they are to profit from it.

Just as adding African American authors to the required reading list in sophomore English classes does not alter the essence of the school culture, building softball fields that are comparable to baseball fields or encouraging young women to enroll in physics classes does not enlarge the culture of schools to be all-inclusive of males and females. While these are important steps to take, all that may be accomplished is the enrichment of the dominant culture in the school. The culture itself is not significantly altered.

Higher education for women remained a highly controversial topic in previous centuries. The prevailing belief was that too much education caused women to become "unfeminine" at least, and incapable of bearing children at most. Nonetheless, by the early twentieth century, there were 110 women's colleges (only about 35 considered the equivalent of men's colleges), and women began to enter publicly funded state universities in greater numbers (Stock 1978). Although resisting admission to female undergraduates until well into the twentieth century (e.g., Harvard in 1969), many of the Ivy League colleges began admitting women to graduate education earlier.

By the beginning of the twentieth century, nearly all public high schools were coeducational (Riordan 1990). Even before the introduction of Title IX in 1972, single-sex schooling at the secondary and higher education levels was increasingly considered irrelevant and counter to the prevailing notion that separate cannot be equal. Furthermore, it was simply too expensive an option for most people.

The rise of the contemporary women's movement, supported by the passage of Title IX, held the mandate of equal access to all aspects of schooling regardless of sex, parallel to the spirit of racial integration. Single-sex schools conflicted with this mandate in principle, if not in direct violation of policy. Nearly all single-sex schools were private, and unless they received federal funds, they were exempted from the dictates of Title IX and not illegal in any sense. But philosophically, to many, single-sex schools represented notions of elitism and separation. Admissions to the schools fell during the 1960s and '70s, and of those that remained open, many either opened admission to students of the other gender or merged with a brother or sister school, creating a coeducational school (Rice and Hemmings 1988).

There is a lingering interest in single-sex education and a considerable body of rather current research on the subject. Some of the literature directly examines issues of academic achievement and socialization, while the other genre of work, feminist theory as it relates to schooling, has established a theoretical framework through which some researchers examine issues of schooling for girls and women. This theoretical framework provides a supporting scaffold upon which arguments can be based for girls-only schooling, either full-time, or part-time as single-sex classes in otherwise coeducational schools.

Reflection on the History

A historical perspective of the education of women tells a story of exclusion and isolation. Once the schooling of females was undertaken in this country, the pattern of inclusion was a sporadic one, with curriculum content being designed to reinforce social, rather than academic, expectations for women. When enrolled in schools, female students were taught those skills necessary for them to carry on in the social roles and were denied power and voice within the broader societal context. In the early twentieth century, separate girls' academies and women's colleges provided the setting for female participation in academic pursuits, but few opportunities existed for women to exercise their educational attainment, whether the curriculum taken was one parallel to that taken by males in their schools or one designed for women, such as that described at Smith College. Coeducation became the norm shortly after the turn of the twentieth century, however, regardless of the opportunity of access, female participation outside of tightly restricted traditional roles remained rare.

The foundation of the initial iteration of the contemporary women's movement was that of equality rather than equity. The outward barriers to full participation by girls and women in both education and occupations, primarily that of access, had to be brought down. In order for full participation to be achieved, females had to be integrated into the male domains. Once that occurred, women's attainment would speak for itself. Being allowed into the male culture would be sufficient for women to gain the knowledge necessary to attain whatever goal they sought. The construct of equality (in this case, simple assurance of opportunity of access) was a critical first step in the process of realizing the authentic participation of females in schools and later in society. It awakened those in charge of running the institutions to the fact that they could no longer grossly discriminate against females.

While equal access to schools has been enforced carefully, the next critical questions have been asked, but not addressed:

Despite equal or nearly equal enrollment in schools, do girls benefit to the same extent as boys?

Gender differentiation in SAT scores, drops in levels of self-esteem, and the degree of participation in classrooms, indicate that they do not.

Is the culture in schools gender-free or even gender-neutral so that girls have an opportunity equal to boys to grow and be nurtured?

Feminist and critical theories recognize the silencing and oppression of classes other than the Euro-male mainstream. And as Bordo (1990) states, females constitute an oppressed class, regardless of their cultural or economic identity. Mann (1996) proposes that under the tenets of the women's movement, we have ignored or resisted the acknowledgment that girls and women are different from males. Because we have feared that by considering there are important differences between the sexes we would cause women to be put firmly back into an underclass, we have hung on to the concept that females must cast off feminine identity, at least outwardly, in order to participate and succeed in male institutions. It would appear there exists considerable evidence that while females can and do achieve well within male-dominated cultures, such as schools, there is a cost of learned silence, loss of a sense of self, and the unremitting battle to fit into a culture other than one's own.

While attempts have been made to equalize the schooling experience for female students, attention has been diverted from developing a better understanding of what girls can gain in settings where they are free to learn within their own culture.

In the chapter that follows, we will explore research that has been undertaken regarding single-sex schooling. In later chapters we will hear the voices of teachers in girls-only classes and hear young women talk about their experiences in girls-only classes and schools.

4

$\mathcal{R}$ecent $\mathcal{R}$esearch

on

$\mathcal{S}$ingle-$\mathcal{S}$ex $\mathcal{S}$chooling

A limited but growing body of literature exists that examines the effects of single-sex schooling on both male and female students. Nearly all of the research employs quantitative designs that focus on traditional outcome measures and generally compares these outcomes to those for comparable students in mixed-sex schools.

Recent Research on Secondary School Students

As posed in Volume II of the 1993 report from the Office of Educational Research and Improvement of the U. S. Department of Education (Hollinger and Adamson 1993), two overriding questions appear to prevail in much of the research:

1. What effect does adolescent subculture (Coleman 1961) have on students in single-sex schools as compared with mixed-sex schools?

2. Moving beyond the initial imperatives of Title IX for equal gender access to schooling, do single-sex schools provide better learning environments for students, especially girls?

In his book, *The Adolescent Society* (1961), Coleman suggested the existence of a culture created by adolescents in schools that represents goals and values at odds with the traditional goal of academic achievement. He found students in coeducational secondary schools tend to be focused on how they look and what possessions they have, rather than on academic achievement. He concluded that coeducational settings empowered the adolescent subculture and negatively affected the formal academic-related school goals. Boys and girls together distract each other. Whether this distraction takes the form of dressing to impress the other gender, competition for teacher time and attention, or sexual harassment, there is no question that distractions exist.

Current research that examines the benefits or drawbacks of single-sex schooling dates from the mid-1980s. As noted earlier, nearly all of these studies rely on quantitative methodology and tend to compare traditional educational outcomes, such as achievement test scores, course grades, and/or career aspirations or attainment. Research in the United States largely focuses on schools in the private sector, generally Catholic schools. This is not surprising in that virtually no public, single-sex schools exist in the United States. The majority of single-sex school research comes from abroad, where single-sex settings are much more common. For example, more than ten years ago, educators in Australia were mandated by the government to show gains in the area of gender equity, and subsequently, policies on teacher promotion became connected in part with implementation of gender-equitable practices. One of the ways Australian schools have chosen to address this issue is through the development of single-sex classes and single-sex schools as options for students in public schools. Other countries, including England, Ireland, and Jamaica, are represented in the research.

In a 1982 study of school environment, Trickett and Trickett, Castro and Schaffner examined perceptions of students in U.S. coeducational and single-sex secondary boarding schools. They concluded that single-sex schools provide climates that emphasize academics significantly more than the coeducational schools.

Riordan (1985) compared academic outcomes of students in Catholic single-sex schools with students in Catholic and public coeducational high schools. He found both boys and girls were advantaged by the single-sex environment, but that girls especially benefited. With the exception of math SAT scores, boys in the Catholic single-sex schools performed better than boys in coeducational Catholic or public high schools. Girls in the single-sex schools demonstrated the highest scores of all groups, outperforming their female and male peers in coeducational schools on nearly all measures. When comparing girls who attended coeducational Catholic schools to those in single-sex Catholic schools, girls in single-sex schools demonstrated higher math scores.

Riordan's 1990 study of outcomes examined gender as well as ethnic group differences in comparing single-sex and coeducational Catholic high schools. His results suggested that single-sex schooling held advantages for white females, as well as male and female minority students. Girls enrolled in the single-sex schools attained higher test scores than girls in coeducational schools, and both African American and Latino students in single-sex schools outperformed their male and female counterparts in coeducational schools.

Lee and Bryk (1986) studied the effects of a single-sex environment on variables such as academic achievement and other school-related behaviors by comparing students during their sophomore and senior years in forty-five single-sex and thirty coeducational Catholic high schools. Their results also indicated benefits for both boys and girls who attended single-sex schools. For example, sophomore boys in the single-sex schools were found to score better in reading, math, and writing, and to be more likely to take math and science classes. Girls in single-sex schools tended to do better in science and reading than girls in coeducational schools, and girls also tended to hold less rigid sex-role stereotypes and higher postsecondary aspirations than their coeducational peers.

As a follow-up investigation to the Lee and Bryk (1986) study, Lee and Marks (1990) attempted to determine whether the previously identified benefits of single-sex schooling carried over into the higher education years. Their findings were that men and women who graduated from single-sex secondary schools tended to be enrolled in more prestigious colleges or universities and were more likely to aspire to graduate school than their counterparts from coeducational high schools. The women from single-sex high schools specifically were found to hold higher educational aspirations than other students in the sample. After controlling for college selectivity, there were no statistically significant carry-over effects of attending single-sex schools over coeducational settings, although there also were no significant advantages connected to attendance at coeducational schools.

Marsh (1989a, 1989b) used a sample similar to that of Lee and Bryk (1986), drawn from Catholic schools that were either coeducational or single-sex. The work investigated the effect of school type on student achievement, attitude, and behavior. After completing a number of analyses, Marsh reported that both boys and girls in single-sex schools were found to have higher reading achievement and a greater number of foreign language and English credits. Marsh also found significant sex-based results in both coeducational and single-sex schools. For example, in comparison to girls, boys had greater achievement growth in math, science, and vocabulary; they chose more math and science courses, and they had greater self-concept in athletics than girls.

The results for girls suggested that their achievement in writing grew more than that of boys, and they spent more time on homework, got better grades, enrolled in more English courses, and reported less stereotypical views of sex roles.

A second study by Lee and Marks (1992) involved a sample of more than 3,000 boys and girls attending independent schools. This sample was particularly important, because previous studies of single-sex education have tended to use Catholic schools for their subjects. In their study, Lee and Marks examined the issue of student choice of single-sex and coeducational schools. Results of the study suggest that a family tradition of single-sex schooling was a stronger influencing variable for girls than boys. The authors also described the constructs of tradition and opportunity structure. They suggest that a tradition structure (on which boys' independent schools tend to be grounded) provides a logical context for male students, because it provides the same expectations and training in which the broader mainstream culture is grounded. Male students in an independent school, whether coeducational or single-sex, can expect to benefit from their schooling because the tradition taught and otherwise reinforced in the school prepares the boys for more of the same after the school years. For boys, the tradition of the school provides the basis for opportunity as adults. However, for girls, the relationship between the tradition structure of an independent school and future opportunity is not as clear.

In this same 1992 study, Lee and Marks suggest that the tradition structure of many independent schools lends itself to preparation of young women for less-than-equal occupational and social status than young men. The authors appear to suppose that independent schooling provides a rather anachronistic status for women—that of second-class citizens—rather than preparing them for opportunities in the modern world. They point out, however, that opportunities for more equal occupational and social status for women are becoming more available.

In their 1994 study of secondary schools, using a sample of classrooms and schools that were independent and non-Catholic, Lee, Marks, and Byrd reported that girls' schools, in contrast to boys' and coeducational schools, were the sites of "pernicious" (p. 1) forms of sexism. In this work, which they describe as one of breadth not depth, their observations from girls' schools suggested to them a tendency for the teachers to "talk down" to the girls, to reinforce hard work rather than correct work, and to create greater dependency in their students when compared to teachers in boys' schools and in coeducational settings. The authors conclude that gender equity practices have the most positive effect on students in coeducational schools (1994). This work is the only major study conducted recently that suggests girls-only groupings may be deleterious to girls.

Steedman (1985) studied the effect of both single-sex and coed schools on secondary-school students in Britain. The results suggested that, in general, boys outperformed girls on the educational outcome measures in chemistry, physics, and math, while the girls did better than the boys in English, French, and biological sciences. However, the results also indicated that both girls and boys in single-sex settings did better in most subjects than their peers in coeducational schools.

Harvey (1985) also sampled students in Britain. This study was intended to examine the effect single-sex and coeducational teaching groups have on science achievement. The 2,900 students were in coeducational schools with single-sex classes, coeducational schools with coeducational science classes, and single-sex girls' and boys' schools. In comparing gender groups in coeducational settings, Harvey found that, in general, there was little difference in academic performance; one exception was that girls in single-sex classes in the coeducational schools did better in physics than those in coeducational classes. Contrary to most other research findings, when science achievement was examined by gender in single-sex and coeducational settings, the results of Harvey's study suggested that girls in coeducational schools outperformed girls in single-sex schools.

Hamilton's (1985) study of Jamaican high school students in single-sex and coeducational schools examined academic achievement by gender and school type. Boys and girls in single-sex schools outscored those in coeducational schools; the overall performance of girls in single-sex schools was the highest, followed by boys in single-sex schools, then boys in coeducational schools, and lastly girls in coeducational schools.

A study conducted in Queensland and Victoria, Australia, (Carpenter and Hayden 1987) focused on girls in their last year of high school, in order to determine the effect of single-sex and coeducational school type on academic achievement. Regardless of controlled variables, no difference was found for girls in Queensland. However, when school type and socioeconomic status were used to explain school type difference, girls in single-sex schools in Victoria outperformed girls in coeducational schools.

One of the few studies that examines middle school students was conducted in Australia by Rowe (1988). Although no vast differences by gender were found, Rowe's results did suggest that students in single-sex classes indicated greater levels of confidence in math. Further, girls who moved from single-sex to coeducational math classes showed a decline in their confidence about their math abilities.

A study conducted in England (Bell 1989) suggested that school type was significant for neither achievement in general, nor achievement by gender. Bell's study, like Marsh's (1989a, 1989b), found that no differences existed in achievement by school type or gender, once selectivity of the single-sex school was controlled.

Conducted with a sample of secondary school students, Cairns (1990) examined more than 2,000 Northern Ireland students in both secondary and academic grammar [elementary] coeducational and single-sex schools for the school type effect on self-esteem and locus of control. He reported that among the categories of cognitive, social, athletic, and general self-esteem, single-sex schools had a positive effect on both self-esteem and locus of control.

Some of the most current data regarding single-sex schooling focused on a girls-only section of a physics class at the Illinois Mathematics and Science Academy (IMSA), a public, state-funded residential high school for talented mathematics and science students. Employing a qualitative design, IMSA (1995) developed and piloted during the 1993–94 academic year an experimental program, offering a girls-only section of calculus-based physics: mechanics. The purpose for establishing the single-sex class was to study whether the girls choosing the single-sex section would acquire greater self-confidence, participate more, and demonstrate higher achievement levels in later science classes than girls who were in the regular coeducational courses. Thirteen girls enrolled in the single-sex section and eleven in the coeducational class. The single-sex section was held during the fall semester, after which all of the girls in that section were placed in traditional coeducational physics classes. Another significant characteristic of the study was that the teacher purposely taught the single-sex section quite differently from the traditional sections. He provided more opportunities for hands-on activities that enabled ". . . students to acquire real-world physics-related experiences which are fundamental to a deeper understanding of advanced physics" (IMSA 1995, 3).

The results of the study suggest that the single-sex setting was a success. More girls enrolled in calculus-based physics: mechanics (single-sex) and the succeeding semester course, calculus-based physics: electricity/magnetism (coeducational) than ever before; the levels of self-confidence of those in the girls-only section were significantly higher than in their female counterparts in the coeducational sections; following participation in the girls-only section, the predictive power of PSAT-M no longer held; in general students in the girls-only section displayed greater growth than other female students in performance on traditional classroom measures, especially in problem solving and analysis; the teacher reported increasing the degree of his reflective practice in response to the dynamics of the girls-only section; and last, the climate of this classroom evolved into a very different one than the other classes. The authors of the study describe the classroom ethos in terms of "a profound sense of responsibility for learning— one's own and each others' learning," "a special rapport between and among the students," which allowed for open exchanges, "a spirit of co-learning," and "strong student influence on classroom dynamics" (IMSA 1995, 2). The one negative effect of the single-sex class reported was that "a few" (IMSA 1995, 2) of the girls in that setting did not like the classroom climate and/or the single-sex construction.

It is interesting to note that despite the overwhelming evidence that supported the single-sex class, the IMSA chose not to continue it beyond the one semester in 1993. "At this time, the Academy does not view single-gender (*sic*) classes as the most appropriate long term 'solution,' and there are no plans to offer single-gender (*sic*) classes next year (1994–95)" (IMSA 1995, 2).

This last study that examined school type and secondary school students used data from the National Educational Longitudinal Study of 1988. LePore and Warren (1997) investigated whether there were academic and social psychological differences, in general and by sex, between secondary students in Catholic single-sex and Catholic coeducational schools. The authors concluded that while boys in single-sex schools showed higher achievement test scores in grades 8, 10, and 12 than boys in coeducational schools, the former did not appear to learn more than their male counterparts. By the end of high school, boys in both groups demonstrated similar growth in achievement test scores. None of the analyses provided results that would support the idea that girls in single-sex Catholic schools were advantaged by school type over the girls in the coeducational Catholic schools, not in achievement scores, self-esteem, nor locus of control. LePore and Warren (1997) speculated that their results were substantially different from previous work, especially that of Lee and Bryk (1986), because of the changing nature of demographics affecting Catholic high schools. The makeup of the student bodies as well as the teaching force has endured considerable change. Minority students and lay teachers are now a much larger part of the Catholic school world than previously. The authors suggest that these shifts, which cause Catholic schools to more closely resemble public schools, may account for school type not being a significant variable.

With regard to their results failing to show benefits for girls in single-sex schools over coeducational schools, LePore and Warren (1997) speculate that increased awareness of gender-equity issues in schools may translate into fewer gender-bias issues for girls, thereby negating the benefits of a girls-only setting.

Recent Research on Post–Secondary School Students

Higher education presents a very different context from secondary schools. Factors such as motivation, economic status, and noncompulsory attendance are just a few of the issues present when comparing the two systems. However, when narrowing the focus of the examination to school type and sex, as has been done in the research on secondary school students, we find that the general picture of research results is as inconclusive for postsecondary education as it is for secondary education.

Riordan (1990) examined a sample of women who attended two or more years of college, and a sample of women who attended four years of college. Among the latter, a small number of these women, (52 out of 2,225) attended women's colleges. Riordan found that women who attended at least two years at a women's college were more likely to go on to postgraduate levels of education and occupations on a higher or more professional level than those in coeducational colleges.

Smith (1990) also studied women at both single-sex and coeducational colleges, investigating educational aspirations, attainment of a college degree, satisfaction with the institution, and perception of the institution's educational goals. Women at the single-sex colleges were found to be more satisfied with 1) their schooling experiences, including counseling and advising, 2) contact with faculty and administration, and 3) the overall quality of instruction. They also were more likely to obtain a degree. In contrast, the women in the coeducational colleges reported greater satisfaction with their social life than the women in the women's colleges.

Tidball has conducted significant research over a number of years regarding the effect of higher education school type on women (1973, 1980, 1985, 1986). The earlier work examined graduates of women's colleges from 1910 to 1940 (1973) and recipients of doctorates from 1920 to 1973 (1980). In both studies, she reported that women who received degrees from women's colleges were more likely to achieve higher distinction in their careers than women from coeducational colleges. In a later study (1986), Tidball narrowed her focus to women with doctorates in science. She reported that women from single-sex colleges found their environment more productive than women in the coeducational colleges. Part of this seems likely to have to do with another finding in her study, which was that there was a positive relationship between the number of women faculty and the number of women working toward a science doctorate.

In a study that examined a number of variables having to do with postsecondary education, Astin (1977) reported findings associated with single-sex and coeducational college attendance by both women and men. A number of positive results were suggested for both sexes in single-sex colleges. The results pertaining to women students were greater opportunities for leadership roles, a greater likelihood of finishing a baccalaureate degree and going on to higher degrees. Astin found that attendance at a men's college was associated with a higher degree of commitment to career plans as well as higher salaries once in the workplace. Both sexes appeared to benefit from greater academic involvement, more interaction with faculty, and higher intellectual self-esteem.

These studies, reflecting the recent research on the effects of single-sex schooling, present a somewhat mixed conclusion, particularly when the research regarding secondary school students is combined with that of higher education students. While the majority of the *qualitative* studies suggest that some and varied benefits exist for students, especially females in single-sex educational settings, the results, based on *quantitative* measures, are not conclusive. Also, rarely part of the discussion is how, if at all, the female-only setting differed from the males' in curricular content or teaching method. We can only assume that in most cases the intent of the teachers was to reproduce for the females exactly what existed in the coeducational or males' classes, at least with regard to the curriculum.

Educators and policy makers have wrapped themselves around the principal of "equal," that is, "the same," for females as males, as the only valid approach to addressing issues that young women have in schools. In other words, they provide exactly the male curriculum and the male pedagogy. But as Mann (1996) fervently believes, Pipher (1994) supports, theory indicates, and much research (e.g., Lewis 1990; Gore 1993; Spender 1982) suggests, traditional secondary schooling experiences and structures are not particularly helpful to girls and young women in building confidence about themselves academically and as maturing young people.

Feminist Theory

Another part of the discussion regarding girls' experiences in schools is feminist theory. Although a number of theorists take substantially different views about the underlying conditions that support their arguments about general social, political, and educational oppression of women, the conclusions are essentially the same. Of those who speak specifically about issues regarding schooling and female students, there is general consensus that most schools support an institutionalized pattern of silencing, which has the effect of denying women the ability to become critical, political, and assertive (e.g., Freire 1993; Giroux 1983; Shor 1980). For further understanding, let's examine the following four theories, or classifications, of feminist theory.

Liberal feminism, often seen as middle of the road, espouses an "equality" approach. It is generally supported by middle-class professional women who tend to have greater economic resources than other groups of women. Equality of opportunity for women is the goal, with one outcome being women assimilated into the world of men, rather than any attempt being made to accomplish the reverse. Given a pluralistic culture, women can organize as a group, successfully compete with other groups for recognition and resources, without a need to radically reconstruct society. Liberal feminism, as supported by the National Organization for Women, for example, calls for the eradication of sexism through the assimilation of women into the social and economic mainstream (Lindsey 1997).

Marxist or socialist feminist theory is founded on Marxism. According to this theory, the subordination of women is directly connected to the capitalist state, which requires the unpaid or underpaid labor force of women in order to function. As the woman remains under the economic domination of her family, and later her husband, she becomes emotionally dependent as well. Men's economic and emotional domination of women, supported by the capitalist system, contribute to women's submission and oppression. Socialist theory suggests that to change the social order, the capitalist system must be dismantled. As posited by Engels, all work, including that connected with the home and children, would be collectivized, thereby freeing women to participate more fully in the general economy (Donovan 1985). Working-class women, less affluent and less satisfied with their current economic lot, are the most likely to subscribe to this view of feminism. Lindsey (1997) suggests that women in Latin America make up the largest group of socialist feminists. She also points out the irony in the fact that women in the former Soviet Union generally have not benefited from social or Marxist theory. Instead, while women are found in the work force, they continue to carry most of the burden for household labor, rendering them saddled with two full-time jobs.

A third classification of feminism is known as radical feminism. Although all proponents don't agree on several pivotal points inherent in this theory, there is agreement with the principle issue: The domination and supremacy of men within the social structure is the root of female suppression and oppression. Radical feminism suggests that the patriarchal family structure creates subjugation of women more than any economic system. Further, it is not possible to have meaningful feminist reform without the creation of a new order, a new set of feminized institutions, which women control. The most radical view contends that all relationships with men, including personal ones, must be severed by women. Unlike liberal feminism, radical feminism does not allow for a woman's integration into the existing social and/or economic construct. And unlike socialist feminism, this theory contends that remaking the economic system into a Marxist one will not accomplish the liberation of women. It is only through women's determination that they are distinctly different from men, and only through their development of parallel and eventually superior social and economic institutions, that their liberation will occur (Lindsey 1997).

A final branch of feminist theory is referred to as multicultural and global feminism (Lindsey 1997). Although not described by Lindsey as definitively as the previous three, one of the major themes of this view is, given an increasingly global and multicultural perspective of the world, artificial and patriarchal-based boundaries, such as those that define countries, must be broached so that all women can be freed from oppression. Womankind will remain oppressed so long as any women remain under patriarchal subjugation.

While each of the aforementioned theories holds distinct views, it can be said that among them there is agreement that feminine gender in and of itself is acknowledged as a classification that is connected with oppression. Many theorists whose work connects issues of feminism and society, identify schools as playing a major role in oppression of females, or at the very least, in supporting unequal and inequitable educational experiences for female students.

Arnot (1982) describes the cultural perspective theory of gender oppression in schools. As students spend time in schools, they become socialized to pervasive gender-role stereotypes taught and modeled in schools, which, in turn, shape girls' and boys' eventual gender identities. These gender identities are taught to the next generation and are reinforced in the schools for each successive generation, because the schools are an integral part and function of the broader society. The adults, both parents and educators, are products of this ideology and the agents by which it is passed on to children. Arnot contends:

> Therefore, what is portrayed is a vicious circle of attitudes in which the learnt attitudes of one generation constrain the new generation and so on. It is in this sense that the concept of "reproduction" is used. (P. 87)

This analysis suggests that issues of gender-differentiated achievement are primarily school-based problems and ones that can be remedied by reconstructing schools in some way. It also suggests that female students as a group tend to experience schooling in much the same way, despite other potentially mediating variables, such as race or class (e.g., Charricoates 1980). The view of a cultural perspective suggests that regardless of girls' race or class, they do not reap the equal or equitable educational benefits that boys do. This appears to be a phenomenon of gender.

The social reproduction theory is based on the premise that capitalism creates schools that reproduce and legitimize social class distinction, preparing students to take "their place" on their appropriate rung of the social ladder. Bowles and Gintis (1976) depict schools as places where students do not have an authentic opportunity to move into positions of higher social status than those from which they have come. Further, schools do not foster the growth of individual self-development, because this notion counters the initiatives of a capitalist society in which the needs of the market place dictate the production of workers (Nicholson 1980). While this theory answers, in many people's minds, questions regarding issues of educational experiences and achievement by social class and race or culture, it does not address gender differentiation *within* a class or race. Are class and race critical variables that affect our experiences in schools? Undoubtedly they are. The central theme of critical pedagogy is that the schooling experience reinforces our acceptance of the dominance of the male and mainstream Euro-centric culture (e.g., McLaren and Leonard 1993). But, as is so often the case, as gender becomes submerged within issues of class and race, the opportunity becomes lost to view gender as a class unto itself. Within each culture, whether oppressed or empowered, the gender hierarchy exists, and males dominate. As we move past the primary question of the early women's movement (How can females access the male-dominated world?), it is important that race and class are understood as critical issues. As hooks (1993) explains:

> Since so many of the early feminist books really reflected a certain type of white bourgeois sensibility, this work did not touch many black women deeply. . . . (P. 150)

Perhaps hooks has it right when she suggests that we should examine sexism through the lens of black women to fully understand the extent of the oppression.

Another important way to understand schools and their differentiated impact on males and females as groups, is to examine the structure and essential values that are the underpinnings of most public schools in the United States. Schools tend to be hierarchical in structure. While school boards were designed to be the policy-making bodies, current research about the function of many school boards suggests that they tend to have little impact on directions taken by schools (Greene 1992). Policy decisions generally are made by superintendents, 95 percent of whom are men (Greene 1992).

Implementation of policy in both elementary and secondary schools then moves to school principals, about 72 percent of whom are male, and teachers, about two-thirds of whom are female (Digest of Education Statistics 1996), who are expected to deliver the policy-based service, and be the direct caregivers. It is evident that despite the longstanding feminization of teaching and the domination of women in the teaching force, the majority of those in positions of power in schools are men, while women tend to be retained in traditional caregiving or teaching roles.

Other aspects of school life reflect what is considered by many to be "male-friendly" to the point of being detrimental to the experiences of females. Perhaps one of the most obvious is the value placed on competition. The early research of Slavin (1983) and Johnson and Johnson (1975) demonstrated the power of collaborative learning structures for all students, regardless of race and gender, in contrast to the traditional competitive pedagogy that appears to empower white male students to the exclusion of other groups.

Despite their findings, most teachers in U.S. public schools continue to reinforce the traditional structure by teaching as they were taught (Arends 1988). This is especially true in secondary schools. Classrooms in high schools have remained, for the most part, teacher centered and textbook driven. Little time is spent in integrating students' knowledge and experience into the *important* content. As Moll (1994) points out, this creates barriers to learning for both males and females who are from cultures other than the mainstream. But because other conditions of the schooling structure exist that are more likely to explicitly empower males, regardless of their culture, the ways students create and understand knowledge can be interpreted as a gender issue that supersedes issues of culture.

Belenky et al. (1986) suggest that the more subtle issues of how schools view knowledge and the knowledge that is chosen as the basis for the schooling experience, are other examples of ways in which female students are valued less than males.

In congruence with both the cultural and social reproduction theories of oppression, traditional schooling cannot be a means of liberation for females, because the essential ways in which males and females understand knowledge is different. Belenky et al. (1986) maintain that the traditional curriculum represents a male view of things that are important, and that the female "way of knowing" is quite different. Cynthia, one of the women in Belenky et al.'s *Women's Way of Knowing* (1986) explained the difference as she saw it.

> Women are concerned with how you get through life from minute to minute. What each little teeny incident—how it can affect everything else you do. Women see things close at hand and are more concerned with minutiae. (P. 199)

The stories of the many women in this 1986 work of Belenky et al. culminate in the theme that females tend to authenticate knowledge that resonates with their own experiences, not that which the researchers characterize as "out-of-context learning" (p. 200), which is what tends to dominate the curriculum in our schools. They associate the latter with a traditional "male way of knowing" that is alien enough to female students to cause a sense of dissonance for women in schools.

One study particularly germane to this point was done by Guinier (1994). The purpose of their study was to determine if, and to what extent, law school experience was a gendered one. This study asked questions beyond the earliest concerns about whether women could succeed in such a male-dominated culture. (Earlier work [e.g., Banks 1988] had questioned whether women law students were too silent or silenced.) Initially, Guinier gathered data from 366 third-year law students at the University of Pennsylvania in 1990. Nearly one half of the respondents (47.5 percent) were female. The survey instrument asked about students' views of gender and their experiences in law school. The study progressed into an examination of student achievement data, including qualitative data, and entailed information from the entire law school student body.

A number of important results were generated from this study. In examining the student achievement data, Guinier found that while men and women, in general, entered the law school with equally high credentials (on some measures, women had higher credentials), women as a group tended to graduate with lower grades. Men were two times more likely to be in the top 10 percent of the graduating class than women, and women tended to earn fewer honors while in law school.

Other gender-specific results were identified. Men were found to be more comfortable than women in speaking with professors of either gender, both in and outside of class. When asked directly, some women students spoke of their frustrations about not seeming able to initiate or maintain satisfactory conversations with professors.

Regarding silence in the classroom, the study found that not only were women far less likely to participate in classroom discussion or voluntarily ask questions, they were increasingly comfortable in their silence. Twenty-eight percent of the first-year women students said they were comfortable with the level of their participation in class. Sixty-four percent of the third-year female students said they were satisfied. The extent of the women's lack of participation did not change over their three-year experience in law school. What had changed was their degree of acquiescence.

One woman cited the law school as "having so few safe places for women" (p. 43) In general, the women who were interviewed during the study, described their law school experiences as gendered and silencing:

> I used to be very driven, competitive. . . . I just stopped trying; just stopped caring. I am scarred forever. (P. 44)

> Talk about a light switch—it went off. It (law experience) just shook my faith, all my self-esteem. (P. 44)

When discussing the academic side of their experiences, men and women interpreted difficulties quite differently. One woman student commented that when women get bad grades they believe it is because they are stupid, while men tend to blame bad grades on the difficulty of law school (P. 44).

Guinier (1994) rejected the idea that their results reflected an isolated case. Instead, they turned to examine the structure of the institution. The competitive nature of the experience and the use of the Socratic method of pedagogy in shaping students into how lawyers ought to be, created a climate for many of the women that produced reactions of silence and disillusion. These women present more compelling stories that coincide with those of the women in Belenky et al.'s (1986) work.

Providing women with the opportunity of access does not speak to the issues of equality that necessarily follow if true equality of opportunity is promised. If silence and increasing alienation tend to be byproducts of women's lives in schools, participation and achievement—regardless of gender—appear to be difficult outcomes to achieve.

Gender Bias in Curriculum, Materials, and Other Areas

There is a considerable amount of literature that unequivocally relates the facts of gendered schooling experiences for students long before they reach undergraduate or graduate collegiate work. The research examines quantitative and qualitative differences by gender in coeducational schools. The areas most frequently examined are curriculum, teaching methods, and teacher interactions.

An early and important study about gender bias in curriculum focused on commercially prepared materials. *Dick and Jane as Victims: Sex Stereotyping in Children's Readers* (Women on Words and Images 1975) analyzed many reading texts used in the United States at the time. This study, as well as others that followed (e.g., Weitzman and Rizzo, 1976; Sadker and Sadker 1982), suggested that texts used in nearly all schools enhanced gender-role stereotyping by failing to include females in stories and illustrations, placing both males and females in unrealistic situations or isolating information about female characters or historical figures in such a way as to show them as irrelevant.

This issue of gender-role stereotyping in teaching materials and texts currently is addressed in the literature much less frequently than twenty years ago. The debate about representation of females in the curriculum appears to revolve more around points concerning what content is delivered as well as the context through which it is presented. For example, a number of university communities have recently debated whether the traditional Euro/male-centric curriculum is the appropriate foundation upon which to base a general or liberal arts education. In addition to this argument is the concern about how the knowledge is presented, beyond issues of behavioral interactions.

Belenky et al. (1986) regard traditional presentation of the traditional curriculum, that is, the common schooling experience, to be at odds with the ways in which females understand and interpret the world. They suggest that schools reflect and are congruent with men's socialization experiences, which are quite different from those of women. Because women tend to construct their knowledge in different ways than men, and because they may value different things, the common teacher-centered schools with Euro/male-centric curricula may present an environment in which female students are less likely to be comfortable than males.

In addition to feminist theory, such as that presented in Belenky et al. (1986), considerable empirical data exist that strongly substantiate the concern about gender bias in favor of male students in commonly used teaching methods. Teacher-centered classrooms, where question and answer periods follow teacher-delivered lectures are settings in which male (especially Euro-American) students are likely to participate more often and more effectively than female students (e.g., Grayson and Martin 1985; Arends 1988). Despite the commonly accepted research results on the power of cooperative learning (e.g., Johnson and Johnson 1994; Slavin 1995), most classrooms continue to be traditionally constructed and operated.

A considerable number of studies have been conducted over the years that have examined gender bias in teacher-to-student interactions in classrooms. As early as 1956, Meyer and Thompson reported classroom research that indicated boys were more likely to receive more positive as well as negative attention from teachers. Over time, these results have not changed. Studies indicate that regardless of the gender of the teacher (Irvine 1986), or the age of the students (e.g., Ebbeck 1984; Fennema and Peterson 1987), male students dominate coeducational settings. Even teachers who consciously work toward gender equity in their classrooms appear to interact with male students more often than females (Streitmatter 1994).

In returning to the two questions asked at the beginning of the chapter, definitive answers do not appear from the research reviewed, particularly that which is quantitative in design. The first question asks: What effect does adolescent subculture have on students in single-sex schools or other single-sex settings as compared with mixed-sex settings? Whether one is a researcher, teacher, parent, or former high school student, it is difficult to deny that adolescent subcultures exist and affect the behavior of adolescents in schools. The question is whether distractions and competition caused by and between the sexes are healthy or appropriate in the school environment, how these two inevitable issues become unhealthy in the form of harassment or denigration of students based on gender, and whether within the coeducational setting students of female culture can fully participate and flourish.

The second question raised at the beginning of the chapter asked: Do single-sex schools provide better learning environments for students, especially girls? Here again, no definitive answer is to be found from the existing literature. In some of the reviewed quantitative studies, achievement scores indicated gains, self-esteem measures were reported as higher, and/or locus of control was higher for girls in single-sex settings. In other studies, no difference was found for girls, and in still other research, boys were found to benefit.

The qualitative-design research seems to lend a slightly clearer focus on the benefits for girls in girls-only settings. The pilot program at the Illinois Mathematics Academy, as well as my own work that follows has the benefit of taking a deeper look into the views of the consumers, that is, the students and the teachers. It is impossible to know if these individual girls would have done differently in coeducational settings than they did in the single-sex groupings. But in the case of IMSA as well as my work, only a few of the girls reported either unhappiness or ambivalence toward their single-sex class experiences. For the overwhelming majority, the girls reported benefiting and enjoying being in class with just girls. It is worthwhile listening carefully to the voices of the girls in these classes before rendering judgment on the efficacy of girls-only learning environments. But first, we will profile the schools, teachers, and classrooms that were observed in this study.

5

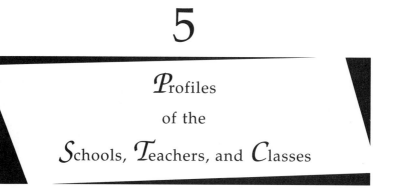

Profiles

of the

Schools, Teachers, and Classes

Presented here is a brief summary of the schools and classes that are included in this qualitative examination of single-sex schooling, as well as some insights to the thinking and backgrounds of principals/administrators and teachers in these schools and classes. As was mentioned in chapter 1, the study includes:

- A private girls school in Connecticut, to which we refer as Connecticut Academy or the acronym CA;

- An all-girls seventh and eighth grade program and a girls-only math class and science class in a middle school in Arizona, which is named Eastside Middle School in this study;

- A girls-only math class in a public Arizona high school, which we are calling Williams High School;

- And a girls-only science class in another public Arizona high school, to be known in this study as Elgin High School.

In reviewing the cases of the girls-only settings, one of the more interesting issues was how the classes came to be.

Connecticut Academy

Certainly a long history and commitment to single-sex education guided the administrators and teachers at this academy.
Although some coeducational opportunities were in place for
the high school-age girls, the school maintained much of its
identity based on the girls-only context.

The issue of support for single-sex classes from the principal at CA was moot. The headmistress was herself a product
of single-sex schools, including college. Further, one of the
chief criteria for working at CA was a strong belief in girls-
only schools, and this would be especially true for the position
of headmistress, who not only administers the school, but also
functions as its head public relations officer.

—◆◆◆—

The single-sex classes in the public coeducational schools were
a very different story. The classes at the different schools were
created through the efforts of local practitioners and in an
almost serendipitous fashion. Further, the degree to which the
classes would become a permanent part of the school appeared
in each case to be based nearly entirely on the dedication of
one or two individuals who were committed to carrying on,
rather than to a systematic analysis of policy followed by the
establishment of a mechanism of institutionalizing the class.

Eastside Middle School

This school had the greatest number of girls-only classes
among the public school sites involved in the study. Beginning
in 1992, the principal established the girls-only seventh
through eighth grade program. Over a period of four years, the
school housed that program as well as another girls-only math
class and science class. The math cohort program came into
being through a somewhat whimsical means.

The principal had come across an article in a newspaper (he
couldn't recall which one) late in the summer of 1992. The
article discussed a girls-only math class in a public school that
had been created to provide a setting where girls might be

encouraged to pursue more math through high school. The principal thought this might be an interesting experiment for his school, inasmuch as his school was a math/science magnet. Moving very quickly, the principal developed the class list, identified the teacher, and began the class within a few weeks from the time he thought of the idea. Not only was there no thought given to teacher preparation with regard to gender issues at the outset, the degree of the principal's support was described as fluid at best by the first girls-only teacher. She described the principal as dictatorial in style, and "once you were on his bad list, you could count on either being totally ignored or harassed." According to the teacher, her relationship with the principal was the former. Whether she really was on his "bad list" was difficult to determine. But it was clear during the four years of observation at the school that the principal paid scant attention to any of the teachers of the girls-only classes. He described his primary concern as that of not being sued for discrimination against boys. Perhaps that was his motivation in staying away from these classes, but his repeated failure to intentionally choose teachers for the girls-only classes who had at least some passing training or interest in gender equity issues suggests that he was simply disinterested so long as problems were not generated by the existence of the classes. Instead, the principal tended to be praised by parents of the girls who participated. To date, each class has a waiting list for enrollment, and although not widely publicized, parents of students at the school like and strongly support the classes. This seems to be due to the ability of the girls to create their own healthy and unique environment, not due to support from the principal, nor to any coordinated efforts on the parts of the teachers.

Williams and Elgin High Schools

The principals of Williams and Elgin High Schools played nearly non-existent roles in the creation of the girls-only math and science classes in their respective schools. In both cases, the teachers were interested in "trying it out" and the principals gave permission. The teachers reported that their principals had not visited their girls-only classes at all during the course of the single year in the case of Williams High, and the two years in the case of the physics class at Elgin High. The physics teacher suggested that there was too much else going on at the school for the principal to worry about just this class. She (the principal) had allowed him to try the class and had faith that it would go well.

Teachers in the Girls' Classes

The range of the various teachers' understanding of and commitment to single-sex schooling was vast. All of the teachers at CA were at least nominally informed about the benefits of girls-only schooling. In the public school classrooms, only one of the teachers observed and interviewed had any previous training in gender-equity issues in schools, and that was minimal. The majority of the teachers involved in the girls-only "experiments" were learning as they went along. On the other end of the continuum were a pair of teachers who taught a girls-only math class at Eastside Middle. The first teacher, a young man, was terminated due to allegations of inappropriate behavior toward some of the girls in the class during the first quarter of the school year. The teacher who followed him was a retired military man who ran the class as much like a boot camp as was possible. Little attention to feminist pedagogy was paid by him. After considering the data from their interviews as well as the field notes from observations of their teaching in the girls-only math class, one could almost assume that the principal, in assigning these two teachers to this class, held a death wish for the class. Neither teacher could ever be assessed as a good teacher in general, and in different ways, each was a terrible choice as a girls-only class teacher. Despite the lack of training or preparation of most of the teachers and the lack of support or benign neglect from the principals, the students as well as the teachers developed strong beliefs about the power of the girls-only climate and how it positively affected the teaching and learning.

Demographics of the Schools

Connecticut Academy

This is an independent, private day school located in an affluent southern Connecticut community of about 60,000. Founded in 1827, it became an all-girls school in 1913. Today it houses grades preschool through 12 and has approximately 670 students enrolled. The annual tuition for the elementary, middle, and high school grades is about $12,000, $13,000, and $14,000, respectively. The school has an endowment of more than $8 million dollars.

The student body is 92 percent Euro-American descent, with most of the minority population described as international. Some financial assistance is available in the way of partial scholarships, and fifty students currently receive this aid. The buildings of the school are set back from a wooded lane a short distance from the town center and next to a boys' school. Beginning about 1970, CA and the brother school began to hold coeducational classes for the high school students in all subjects other than math. For example, during the 1995–96 school year, students at the schools could take chemistry at CA or the boys' school, although physics was offered only at the boys' school. But despite the offerings of coeducational classes, the administrators, teachers, and students spoke of the schools as single-sex.

If the literature on the table next to the CA's receptionist's desk is any indication, those connected with independent girls' schools are at least fairly knowledgeable about the research and attendant issues regarding girls and their experiences in coeducational public schools. In fact, the possible benefits garnered by girls in single-sex settings is highlighted as the primary sales pitch.

Among the literature found in the outer office was a brochure, *Choosing a Girls' School,* published in 1995 by the National Coalition of Girls' Schools, which presents a listing of the seventy-five member schools, and is sprinkled with pictures of girls in various school activities along with bulleted points such as:

- Girls at girls' schools are always at center stage.
- Everyone has a voice in the classroom.
- The "can-do" atmosphere at a girls' school yields life-long rewards.
- Four times as many graduates of girls' schools intend to pursue careers in math, science, and technology.
- Almost 80 percent of the recent alumnae surveyed cite their single-sex school experience as pivotal in preparing them for productive personal and professional lives.

Several days' observation, during the fall and spring terms of the 1995–96 academic year, and interviews with the school administrative staff and several teachers, revealed classrooms where teachers taught in traditional ways. There was neither an indication nor a report of any specific pedagogy or curriculum that reflected special attempts to educate the girls in ways other than those typically associated with most classrooms. Classrooms were teacher- and text-centered, students who raised their hands in class were called on to answer teacher-initiated questions, and science and math lessons were exactly what one would expect to find in any college prep middle or high school classroom. Here there was no critical pedagogy, no cooperative learning, no feminist curriculum.

Clearly, this school relies on the history, tradition, and strong culture of the school to elicit the outcomes espoused in the pamphlet. According to school personnel, girls educated together create a sufficiently powerful culture that by itself empowers girls. To "water down" the curriculum (teach anything other than what the boys at the neighboring school are being taught) or to instruct in ways other than those that are considered traditional (again, in comparison to the boys' school, which represents the classical prep school curriculum and pedagogy), is to give the girls less and therefore victimize them. Tightly woven into the culture of this girls' school is the socioeconomic class of the girls, and the town in which they live. According to the demographic information provided by the school, whether the girls are of the small minority or dominant majority population, they are of upper-middle or upper class, and nearly always go on to highly competitive colleges and universities. They probably would do so whether they had attended CA or not, consistent with nearly all of the research that connects higher levels of socioeconomic status with higher levels of educational achievement and occupational attainment (e.g., Clabaugh and Razycki 1990). But simply because the graduates of CA reinforce the quantitative research by virtue of their socioeconomic status, does not mean the individual girls who attend CA do not benefit from, and value, the single-sex experience.

-◆◆◆-

The three coeducational public schools in this study are all located in a southwestern city of 750,000 that is approaching 40 percent minority population, with Latino representing the largest minority group. Because each setting is so different, descriptions of the schools are important and follow in the order in which each classroom was added to the study.

Eastside Middle School

Eastside is located in a middle-class neighborhood with a predominantly Euro-American population. It serves as a math/science magnet school, drawing slightly less than one-third of its students from minority neighborhoods, many of which are poorer than the school's neighborhood.

As mentioned earlier, the school principal organized the girls-only class, based on a newspaper story he read late in the summer of 1992 about a girls-only class on the East Coast. He believed that it was an interesting means of addressing gender differentiation in achievement in math, and decided to organize one at his school. The teacher was informed of her selection to teach seventh grade, girls-only pre-algebra barely two weeks before the opening of school. She decided that she would teach the same curriculum as she would any pre-algebra class, but would enhance the concept of a girls-only group by having women in role-model positions provide seminars for the girls throughout the year. As an invited speaker, this was my first introduction to this class.

During the first year of this class, twenty-four girls were enrolled. Their initial enrollment was not voluntary. Instead, the principal, wanting to do everything he could to ensure success, chose incoming seventh graders who had histories of doing well in math and scheduled them into the class. The teacher related an interesting anecdote during a conversation about the first day this all-girls class met. One student raised her hand and asked, "Where are the boys?" The teacher responded, "I guess you're right. There aren't any boys. Is that all right with you?" The girl said, "Oh, yes!" and a number of the other girls shouted: "All right!"

During the first quarter of that school year, all of the girls' parents were notified that the class was an all-girls experiment, and during Open House, those parents who attended were very enthusiastic. At the end of that school year, one girl chose to enter a coeducational math class for eighth grade, one had moved, and four new girls were added to the class. The group of twenty-six, twenty-two of whom had been together in the seventh grade pre-algebra class, moved as a cohort with the same teacher into an eighth grade algebra class.

Of the twenty-six students in the eighth-grade class, fourteen were chosen to be interviewed during the course of the year. Two were African American, two were Latina (among these four, one from each of the ethnic categories was a magnet transfer student from a low socioeconomic neighborhood), two were Asian American (one a magnet student), and the rest were of European descent and middle class.

Elgin High School

Elgin High is a comprehensive high school, although it emphasizes a college preparatory curriculum. Approximately 80 percent of the 1,800 students go on to some type of higher education. It is located in a middle-class, predominantly European-descent neighborhood.

In the spring of 1994, a doctoral student with whom I was working expressed an increasing interest in gender issues in science education. He had taught physics and chemistry at

Elgin High for more than twenty years, and as he worked on a dissertation about students and their perceptions of physics, the issue of girls' achievement and attitudes compared with those of boys began to interest him. He decided that developing a girls-only physics class at Elgin High might provide some interesting outcomes with regard to both achievement and attitudes. During class registration for fall 1994, thirty-three girls enrolled in the experimental girls-only physics class, while fourteen enrolled in the coeducational physics class that was taught by the same teacher.

During the 1994–95 school year, interviews with sixteen girls were conducted, the class was observed about once every ten days, and conversations with the teacher were held periodically. During the summer of 1995 and again in the fall of 1996, follow-up interviews were conducted with seven of the former students in the physics class. Of the original thirty-three students, one was African-American, four were Latina, and the remainder were of European descent. One Latina and six European-descent students were located for the follow-up interviews.

Williams High School

Williams High is the oldest high school in the city. For the past several years, it has been designated as a science and math magnet school with the intent being that students of European descent would transfer to the school to participate in the specialized curriculum. However, of the approximately 2,400 students, its enrollment remains primarily minority, with 57 percent Latino/a, 6 percent African American, 3 percent Native American and Asian, and the remaining 34 percent of European descent. The community from which the majority of the students come is socioeconomically under- and lower class. The school reports that approximately 60 percent of the students go on to some form of postsecondary training, with the majority of those going on to college enrolling at the local community college.

During the fall of 1995, a math teacher and a special education teacher opened a girls-only math class. This class was developed as a remedial Algebra I class for girls who had failed at least one math class in high school. In addition, approximately one-third of the students were identified as mainstreamed, special education students who needed special attention in order to succeed in math. All of the girls in the class had been placed there, rather than voluntarily enrolling. By the middle of October, the class had stabilized at twenty-one students. Both teachers worked together in the class, with the math teacher providing the majority of the formal instruction and the special education teacher providing individual attention to the students requiring it.

The girls in this class presented a very different picture from those in the other public school, girls-only classes. All of them were of color, either Latina, African American, or Native American, and all were from poor families. In addition, a number of them were not primary English speakers. However, despite the differences of age, socioeconomic class, and cultural background, among the girls in the various girls-only in this study, many of the same themes appeared throughout all of the interviews.

With brief profiles of the schools, teachers, and students in this study established, we will proceed in the next chapter to hear the *voices* of the teachers who were dealing with the issue of girls-only vs. coed classes. Subsequently, the students in the girls-only classes will reveal their feelings about their school experiences.

6

*V*oices

of the

*T*eachers

D uring the course of the study, a number of teachers
were interviewed (Appendixes A and B) and observed
working in girls-only classrooms as well as in mixed-
gender classes, where they taught the same subject. The purpose in doing this was several-fold: first, to get a sense of the
teacher's general approach to teaching, discipline style, and
interaction patterns with students; second, to observe whether
the teacher appeared to work differently with the girls-only
compared with the mixed class, and third, to observe how the
dynamics within the girls-only classes unfolded, given the
teacher's actions.

The teachers presented in this chapter represent a broad
spectrum of teaching experience, knowledge of and commitment to gender issues, and teaching expertise. Mr. Paul of
Connecticut Academy was the most experienced teacher and
the most knowledgeable of issues involving girls and schooling. He also was one of the best teachers in a general sense.
Mr. Gordon was the least experienced, having only substituted
for two years, had the least amount of information about gender issues, and with the exception of Mr. Lincoln, could be clas-
sified as the least competent teacher. The other teachers fell in

various places on the continuum between these two teachers who represented the extremes.

Connecticut Academy

Mr. Paul has been a teacher at Connecticut Academy for twenty-six years. During the whole of that time, he has taught science, and during the past six years has been in the middle school. Not surprisingly, among all of the teachers interviewed during the course of the study, he was the most well-versed on the subject of girls-only schooling, and in fact has published several articles on the subject of girls and science. He talked about his support of girls being in single-sex classes for math throughout their secondary schooling, and in science through the eighth grade; exactly the structure used at CA. He described his perceptions of some of the benefits:

> I've read some research that was done in England in the late 1970s, and what they found was something that's been reinforced since, that if we separate boys and girls in science through about 8th grade, and math through about the British equivalent of about our junior year, the girls do much better. So as we do here, you can have a girls school and combine some of the classes, or in a public school have a coed school and separate some of the classes, and I think that might be a bit easier to handle.
>
> [I think the girls'] abstract thinking is different, or they're able to make associations differently [than the boys]. I discovered when I taught 9th-grade biology, if I taught to the boys I would lose the girls immediately. And we also know that in a single-sex school, the girls benefit while the boys may not. If we have a coeducational school, the boys benefit.

Mr. Paul also talked about benefits other than academic. Much of the literature advertising CA speaks to the issue of the development of leadership skills for young women in single-sex schools, and his comments echoed the CA literature as well as the research literature:

It benefits the girls to separate them in academic areas, and I think we give more girls more leadership experiences, and something that we don't really think about a great deal, but more effective *followership*. I don't mean *passive sheep*. I mean really effective followership opportunities. We increase their confidence, and I think we increase their ability to articulate their thoughts.

Eastside Middle School

Ms. Mary was in her first year of teaching at Eastside Middle when the girls-only math program began. Although she had taught math for seven years at a high school on the far west side of the city, she was nervous about doing well at her new school and was very uncomfortable with her assignment as the teacher of this experimental class. She also was uncertain about whether she even agreed with the concept of isolating girls in a math class:

I was a math major as an undergrad. I had mostly men in my classes, and I succeeded. I didn't have any special treatment, and I think it's important for people to make it on their own.

[When I started the year] I was afraid it was going to be illegal, and then I was afraid that I didn't know enough about gender issues in general to even be successful as it was.

By the end of the first year of the girls' math program, Ms. Mary's doubts were significantly allayed. She described the girls in her class at the end of that year:

They were more willing to take risks, and they were more willing to be responsible. They'd always excite me; sometimes they would make these jumps that my other classes couldn't or wouldn't make, and that always made my day because, you know, that's what you look for. You look for those little leaps that kids make. And they would do it at least once a week if not more, and so I used to feel very good about the class because I thought, "Okay, this is what's supposed to be happening." They seemed much more positive about math than girls in my other classes. They seemed much more goal-oriented and it made me feel like, "Well, maybe I was wrong; maybe this is a good thing; maybe even if it's illegal we should still do it."

During her time teaching the girls-only math program, conversations were periodically held with Ms. Mary on various topics related to the class. Throughout, she was asked about her view of differences and similarities in how she taught that class compared with her mixed-gender classes. In the beginning, she was adamant that not only was her *intention* to teach the same in every situation, but that she did so. As time went on and she thought about the field-note data that clearly conflicted with her own perceptions about her teaching style in the girls-only class, she began to acknowledge that the girls-only environment made a difference not only to the girls, but also to her in how she taught. At the end of the third year, she said:

> I know now, after I've given it a lot of thought, that I do work with the girls-only group differently than the other mixed group. I really believed I didn't, but now I see that I do. The girls bring out more in me while I try to bring out more in them. I'm just as tough on them, maybe tougher, but it's different. And it's not as if their behavior is any better than the boys and girls in the other classes. They're really chattier than other groups. But I know that I don't have to spend energy ignoring some of the really immature behavior of some of the boys. And I don't have to work so hard drawing out the girls. In the girls-only class, they draw themselves out. It's very different. And I know I teach differently too. The questions we get into allow me to concentrate more on process. I really don't know why.

By the end of the three years of teaching girls-only math at Eastside Middle, Ms. Mary held clear and strong opinions

about the positive aspects of her single-sex class. Her perceptions were perhaps best illustrated by the fact that she registered her own daughter, then in the seventh grade in this
school, in the girls-only math class for the following year, when
Ms. Mary would be teaching at another school.

Mr. Lincoln and Mr. Gordon shared the teaching year of the
girls-only math class the year after Ms. Mary left. Mr. Lincoln,
a young teacher who had been transferred to Eastside after
two years' experience at a far west side high school, began the
school year with twenty-five girls. The principal had not provided him with any guidance about the girls-only class, nor
had he had any conversations with Ms. Mary about the class,
even though her daughter was in his class. He described him-
self as having an interest in single-sex education, because he'd
gone to a men's college for two years; however, when asked his
opinions about any of the research or popular literature on the
subject, he was at a loss. He did describe the girls-only class as
different from his other classes in several respects:

> For me it's more playful. For them [girls], it's more play-
> ful. They like me, probably more than the other classes.
> It's a little kinder, which is nice. For me, being playful is
> really nice. It's really, I like to be that way, that's more my
> personality. I think I get to see, I think they get to show
> in some ways different parts or more of themselves than
> they would in a normal class. I get the sense that the
> girls pay more attention in class and it's easier to get the
> instructions across.

When asked if he thought he taught this class in the same
way as he taught the others, he said, "I play things by ear,
but I use the same textbook." Playing things "by ear," not
being able to control the behavior in his classes, and a charge
from the parents of one of the girls in the girls-only math
class that he was too familiar and "touchy" appeared to create the basis for his termination from the district early in the
school year.

Mr. Gordon, a frequent substitute teacher at Eastside, was hired to take Mr. Lincoln's place for the remainder of the year. Mr. Gordon believed that his attention to stricter discipline in comparison to Mr. Lincoln was one reason he had been asked to take over the position. Mr. Gordon also believed that, due to his long experience in the military, he was suited to teach middle school. Further, when asked about his previous experience or training in issues of gender equity, he felt quite confident that he was quite prepared.

> When I got this class, I didn't know anything about why it had been set up this way, and I really still don't. But I can say that I had a lot of training during my military career in gender awareness. We had mandatory classes on racial relations, then after racial relations, when the women's movement became very big, then we had classes, I had probably 30–40 hours of formal training on gender bias and how to deal with it both as a supervisor and all of that stuff. And here it doesn't seem to be a big deal. But I like equal opportunity.

Mr. Gordon had some strong opinions about how to organize the class for the future, whether he was to continue as the teacher or not.

> Get rid of the kids who don't want to do math. Take Sonya. She doesn't want to learn. I'm wasting my time with kids like her. Make this class an elite.

When asked if he thought the class might be useful for girls who were having trouble in math in coeducational classes, he allowed as how this might be the case, but he didn't particularly want to spend his time dealing with students for whom motivation might be an issue. He continued:

> I still say you can stick Sonya and others like her in any class and they'll fail no matter what. We need more of a selection process.

Sonya and one other girl were having problems in this class. They didn't do the homework, failed the tests, and in general seemed to retain their difficulties from the time Mr. Lincoln was the teacher. One of them was the student who lodged the complaint of unwanted attention against Mr. Lincoln. Shortly after the winter break, both students had been removed from the class at Mr. Gordon's insistence. Despite Mr. Gordon's unwillingness to work with students who presented the greatest challenges, he still maintained a strong belief in the girls-only structure, although this was confounded by his strong belief in being able to do great things because he was the one doing it.

> Give me this special class [selection based on strong motivation] of girls for a year and I'll bring them ahead of any class in the school. You give me this group, and I'll have them doing algebra by the time the year's over. And I don't care if they failed sixth-grade math. I'll have them doing it.

—◆◆◆—

Ms. Louise had taught at Eastside Middle School for three years. Just before the beginning of the 1995–96 school year, she had been assigned by the principal as the teacher of a girls-only section of eighth-grade science. When asked about her background and interest in gender issues, she said:

> Gender equity is an interest of mine. That's why I have a Girl Scout troop. I started when my daughter entered Scouts. The only formal training I've had was an in-service [staff development session] at the other school where I taught.

Ms. Louise also remarked about the effects she perceived from a girls-only setting:

> The girls need to have their own environment. With the [girls-only] class, they don't have to compete with boys, and maybe they'll come out and do better with science. In

the Scout troop and the class, I saw that the girls were really timid in the beginning. But now, they're really outspoken. Even when they're with boys now they speak their minds.

The other topics that came up in the interview had to do with Ms. Louise's perceptions about her teaching methods in this class and how she felt the girls were doing in comparison with the female students in her other classes.

There are thirty-three girls in this class. It's my biggest one. There are about twenty-four boys and girls in the other classes. All of the girls volunteered to be in there. I try to teach this class the same way I do my other ones, but it turns out to be different. So far I've seen that they don't have to fight. They seem to give and take and they're nice to each other. Of course they don't share during a test, but otherwise they're willing to help each other. They seem just as competitive as the other students, but when they're concerned about a friend getting a higher grade, they seem to think, "How can I make it better?"

It has been very friendly, congenial. They feel comfortable bringing anything up. There's no such thing like "Somebody's going to hear me say something bad or stupid." They have free thinking here and there's no stifling.

There's almost 100 percent homework turn-in rate. In the other classes, I guess the girls don't see that girls can do it. I push the girls in the other coeducational] classes, but it seems to me that there is a lot of comparison with the boys. In the girls-only class, there's not much of an attendance problem and no discipline problem. As a teacher, I'm more relaxed. I don't have to stand on guard all of the time. I don't have to control the boys who are the ones who call out all of the time. In those classes, the girls kind of just sit and let the boys call out and get the attention. In those classes, the timid girls are just more timid and end up not participating much or at all.

I thought in a girls-only class that there were going to be a lot of pushy girls. But there's no pushy stuff. The girls respect each other much better than in a mixed class.

Ms. Louise discussed considerable differences between her girls-only and coeducational classes. She believed that the girls worked to create a unique climate where they achieved to a greater extent than the girls in the coeducational classes. Further, the girls nudged the teacher into different ways of teaching—ways that were more collaborative than in other classes. Lastly, Ms. Louise spoke of one of the effects on the students of being with just girls. According to her, the girls, who she anticipated would have demonstrated "pushy" behavior, worked together and supported one another in a respectful climate:

> My experience with girls-only has been tremendous. I've seen a difference in the girls in my troop and in this class. They were timid in the beginning—now they're really outspoken and can speak up even when they're with boys.

Elgin High School

Mr. James, the teacher of the girls-only physics class at Elgin High was a veteran teacher of twenty years, all of which were at this school. He became interested in teaching a girls-only physics class during the time of his dissertation research. He created the class, with the permission of the principal, as an interesting experiment. During registration the previous spring, thirty-two girls registered for the girls-only section, and fourteen registered for the coeducational section. From the beginning, Mr. James was a bit nervous about how things would turn out; however, he was clear on the point that he would teach the same way and the same things to each of his physics classes:

> I don't want anyone to be able to say that what goes on in this class is any different, that the girls might not be getting as good an experience as they would in the other class.

Toward the end of the first of two years that Mr. James taught this class, he indicated he believed there were some critical differences in how the girls did in the girls-only class, compared with how both girls and boys did in the coeducational section.

> The girls in here get their work done. And they seem more focused. That's probably because there aren't any boys to distract them, because I don't think this group is necessarily any brighter than the other group. And an amazing number of them are getting As. The grades in here are higher than any other group I've ever taught. I don't have discipline problems in any of my classes, so I can't really compare that issue. I do think that if a girl wants a girls-only section in physics, or maybe math too, that it should be an option. There's no way of knowing for sure if these girls would have done as well without the girls-only class, but I think it has made a difference for some of them.

Williams High School

Ms. Grace and Ms. Quinn team-taught the girls-only class at Williams High. This class was designed for low-achieving and mainstreamed special education students. The curriculum for the class was a combination of integrated math and algebra. The teachers referred to the class as a foundations course. Most of the girls were either juniors or seniors who needed the math credit to finish high school. None had succeeded in her math class the previous year. Ms. Grace explained:

> We run a foundations class every year. We requested an all-female group last year, but it never came to be, so again we asked for it this year. They promised it would be done. We have some girls who requested the all-girls section, and some who didn't.

Both teachers talked about their own interests in creating this class. Ms. Grace said:

> I am a female in a field that was very much dominated by males. I have felt the difference of being a female in a

male-dominated field in non-positive ways. I've been wanting to do something like this for years. What I've been doing up till now is just making sure I encourage females in my honors classes to strive in math and science. So this was a new approach to attack the problem.

Ms. Quinn offered this:

As a special education teacher there's a disproportionate number of boys in special ed, so most of my self-contained classes are mainly boys, and I've seen the high failure rate of girls in these math classes. I've tried to examine what we have to offer the students that's unique, besides having two teachers in the room, and coming up with an all-female class was something that we could offer the students.

The two teachers then talked about the dynamics they saw in this class. One of them commented:

For a little while, we had boys in here because of a scheduling mess-up. During that time, I did some informal observations and noticed whenever [the team teacher] would do the group teaching, that almost all of the time the boys would respond and give all the answers in class and the girls would say absolutely nothing. Even when we told the class that this was going to be an all-female class and the boys were going to be moving, the girls still didn't say anything. It was only the boys who responded.

Another of their comments:

I don't think I'm any less sympathetic to boys. But I do know that it doesn't feel good to be told that you're not capable of knowing this just because of who you are. So, I tend to be more nurturing to the girls and try to pull things out of them that they don't know they're capable of themselves sometimes. I want them taking as much math as possible and being successful in it.

Both teachers felt strongly that through the girls-only format, they could give their students more than academics. Personal issues that many of the girls at Williams High deal with were ones interjected throughout the conversations with the teachers, as well as the students in the class.

Among the teachers' comments:

There are some issues we discuss with the students. Teen-age pregnancy, it's a big problem with this clientele. Battering is an issue too. So there are topics we discuss in here that I've never discussed head-on in other classes. Last Tuesday, we showed a film on women heroes. We had them do a writing assignment ahead of time, writing about women heroes they have, and very few had any they could name. Most mentioned their mothers, and that's a start, but I mean this role-model issue, trying to put prominent women in front of them, it is a definite goal. But mainly, having them be comfortable and let them realize that there are cultural things there that they need to work against. We see this class as a real opportunity to create change for some of these girls, and we never intended to try to teach this class the same as any other.

—◆◆◆—

Each of the teachers of the girls-only classes presented a distinct profile, both with respect to the general quality of their teaching, as well as their understanding of and commitment to gender issues in their teaching. Mr. Paul of Connecticut Academy, Ms. Mary of Eastside Middle, Mr. James of Elgin High, and Ms. Grace and Ms. Quinn all were described by their principals as excellent teachers. Ms. Louise was described as a fairly new teacher who was doing well and had potential to be very good. Mr. Lincoln was terminated mid-year and clearly had major difficulties in both his teaching ability as well as his judgment in how he related to his female students. And Mr. Gordon would perhaps be considered by some to be a good teacher, especially if one tends to appreciate a dictatorial style.

The Eastside Middle principal had confidence in him. Field-note data from our observations in their girls-only, as well as other classes they taught, confirmed the assessments of the principals, with the exception of Mr. Gordon. Observations of him created a strong impression of a person with an over-whelming concern with discipline and a need to be in total control. This tended to translate into an unwillingness on Mr. Gordon's part to allow much conversation among the students and only occasional group work specifically, and little freedom in the classroom in general.

—◆◆◆—

Although the settings of the three coeducational public school classrooms at Eastside Middle, Elgin High, and Williams High are those that are profiled throughout this study, other classes at Eastside Middle were analyzed in the course of data collection. One was a girls-only eighth-grade science class in its first year of operation, and another was a seventh-grade, girls-only math class, which was the beginning of the second iteration of the cohort begun by Ms. Mary during the 1993–94 academic year.

During the course of the interviews with these teachers, as well as the teachers of the profiled classes, it became clear that although the range of preparation for teaching in a girls-only context varied, as did the degree of commitment to gender issues, a theme of the importance and the uniqueness of a girls-only setting arose among all of the teachers. And despite the variation in "teacher quality" in the varied classes, they tended to believe that the girls did better academically than they would have in a coeducational setting, that a different cli-mate was created that was positive, and in most of their cases, even that of Mr. Lincoln, they tended to believe that the girls felt freer to be themselves.

7

$\mathcal{V}$oices of $\mathcal{G}$irls

in the

$\mathcal{P}$rivate $\mathcal{S}$chool

S usan and Kathy, a seventh and an eleventh grader respectively, were selected at random to be interviewed (Appendix C). Both were happy to spend some time discussing their school and revealing a bit about their lives. The girls may be considered representative of others enrolled at Connecticut Academy, which I refer to as CA in this study. Both girls were of European descent, from affluent families, and had lived in the area all of their lives. They were students in a classic girls-only setting, an old prestigious New England girls' school, and I was curious to see if their perceptions of their experiences at CA matched the school's printed promotional material, *Choosing a Girls' School,* which (as noted in chapter 5) is based on results of a research effort (National Coalition of Girls' Schools 1995).

Did Susan and Kathy see benefits from being at a girls-only school? Further, because Connecticut Academy is to some extent coeducational in the upper school, how did they feel about the inclusion of boys in those grades?

Interview With Susan

Susan, a seventh grader, had attended Connecticut Academy since Kindergarten. She is the oldest of five children, all of whom attended private schools. Her father had commuted from Toronto on the weekends for the past three years, and Susan thought there might be a possibility that the family would move to Toronto at the end of the next year so they could live together again.

During the interview, she shimmered with energy. She was enthusiastic about everything, quieting only for a moment when several older girls came into the eighth-grade lounge, which is normally off-limits to the younger girls. She was distinctly uncomfortable about intruding on their territory, and when the older girls left, her energy level picked up immediately. The interview began with Susan saying what she liked about CA:

> I like going to an all-girls school 'cause there are things I do that I probably wouldn't do if there were guys here. I don't always do my hair and like that. I can just be myself.

We broadened the discussion to Susan's perceptions of the school, and she talked about the girls and her classes.

> Our grade used to be a lot of groups, but now it's not like that. I don't have anyone in the grade who I don't like or doesn't like me. I'm not like in a group. I just drift to different ones. That's good. I don't just have to be in one group, 'cause it's not like that.
>
> My favorite subject changes a lot. Last year it was History. This year it's Honors Math, at least I think it's Honors Math. Right now we're doing trig and I like it a lot. Another reason I like math is that my mom is like, "Right now, girls stop liking math and science." So I like math. I like Latin too.
>
> Here you never have math with boys, which I think is good. My mom has all these books, and I read them to see what they think I'm supposed to be like, and they talk

about in math where the boys are always overpowering girls. I'm glad to not have had boys in class, but I'm looking forward to other classes with boys in high school. Except for math that I want to keep separate, it probably won't be any different.

Susan's mother featured prominently throughout the conversation. Some of her aspirations and fears for her daughter were clearly defined in Susan's mind.

My mom has *Reviving Ophelia* [Pipher 1994]. That one was a little dramatic. My mom doesn't really read the books, she just gets them. I read them though. I do so I can see if I'm having all these problems I'm supposed to be having. But I'm not really that far into being a teenager. I just turned thirteen in March. I can't really measure myself now.

When asked whether she saw herself going to a coeducational college, Susan giggled and then emphatically said "Oh yes." She went on to intertwine her mother's aspirations for her into her own experiences.

My mom says she thinks it's better to go to a coed college. She says that part of the college experience is like dating and everything. Both my parents went to Brown and met there. But my mom went to all-girls schools before college.

I think when I was like five, my mom read all these studies about how girls learn better in a single-sex environment, so my mom thought it would be better if I went here, so here I am.

Susan's mother, and in turn Susan, were both clear about the benefits of girls-only schools for Susan. As an effervescent thirteen-year-old, she valued the club-like culture of the all-girls environment, and, at the same time, she looked forward to being with boys in college. Because it was her mother's issue, she thought about the importance of having math with only girls, although she hadn't thought about coeducation classes beyond that.

Interview With Kathy

Kathy, poised, articulate, and quiet, was a junior at CA. As was the case with a small number of other girls at the school, she commuted from a nearby, just slightly less affluent, community. She too is one of five children, the second oldest. She came to CA from a private, coeducational middle school in her own town. Her parents felt the quality of education was better at CA than her previous school, so she transferred in the ninth grade.

When asked about her perceptions of CA, especially compared to her coeducational public school experiences, she answered:

> I never thought there would be much of a difference being in an all-girls school, but I find it gives you a chance to be yourself. I've always had great guy friends, and so I thought I'd miss having the guys around, but you have the balance, like in the lounge [where boys are allowed to visit]. Although it's generally girls, because not too many guys are here often. Girls here just don't hold things back. They don't have to be afraid to say something in front of a guy. The environment is really more free.

While CA and its adjacent brother school are described by students and adults as single-sex schools (and this is true in every sense at the lower and middle schools), both schools hedge their bets by offering coeducational classes to high school students.Kathy's comments took another direction when I asked how she felt being with boys in some of her classes.

> All my classes except math are with guys. There's a little bit of difference with them in there, but I don't feel it restricts me. I would have asked the question whether there was a guy in there or not. There isn't as much difference in the classes as in the lounge.

I asked Kathy to talk especially about her physics class, which was located on the boys' campus.

My teacher is a young man and really cool. I feel the guys come to class in a joking-around manner, because they feel they can do that with this young teacher. I feel it's mainly the girls who ask the questions and if they do ask a question it's just as equally looked at. The guys have a tendency more to just write down what the teacher says and not worry about it then. But they worry about it right before the test. The guys don't do the homework until the night before the test. And then they have all these questions. For me it's kind of distracting to hear their side comments. The things they say are just stupid. The girls feel really pressured. Basically the left side of the room does that. It's really separated [girls and boys]. All my science classes the past years have been like that. But the guys who do sit on the right side of the room are like super physics students and ask questions that we [girls] have no clue about. The teacher clicks on it right away. It's a definite separation between the two [girls and boys].

Kathy barely paused before she went on to explain how she felt about going to the boys' school for this class.

At first I was scared. My pet peeve is walking the foot path alone. I was so scared to walk it alone. When you walk up to the school, there are these high windows, and you look up and all these guys are peering down at you. But it's come to the point, having two classes over there, that I don't even care any more. I don't ever go into the lounge over there, though.

It is interesting to note that there were only eleven students in Kathy's physics class, yet she very clearly had constructed lines of demarcation by gender and ability. The boys were either lazy or careless and made "stupid" comments, or they were the best and the brightest in the class. She portrayed the girls as hard working but none of the four of them fell into the high-achieving group in her mind. Although she was achieving A and B grades in the class and considering whether to take advanced physics or chemistry during her senior year, she did not see herself as doing so well in the class.

To some extent, students were separated by gender, as Kathy remembered all of her previous science classes to be, but perhaps more importantly, the teacher *clicked* on the smart boys. In addition to her experiences in the class, she felt intimidated just walking into the boys' school. Kathy feared the lounge at the boys' school and sought the refuge of the lounge at CA.

There were a number of issues Kathy was struggling with, none of which had to do with learning physics. Nevertheless, when I asked her if she would prefer to take a physics class at CA, she said that the teacher at the boys' school was so good, that she would choose his class wherever it was located. This seems consistent with the reasoning of the school administrators. The CA headmistress explained that mixed-gender classes are provided in order to take advantage of the expertise of the instructors at each school, to provide the students with a choice, and to provide a transition from the single-sex isolation to the coeducational world.

All of these issues are important considerations, and yet Kathy's words are troublesome. She is a serious and high-achieving student, and yet she contends daily with feelings of alienation, or in the case of walking the foot path, fear, just to get to the class. She also feels that, despite her initial indication that boys in the class made no difference, she cannot or does not compete well with the super physics students. Another interesting point is that she doesn't speak of the boys as individuals, but rather as two groups who are either distracting and poorly behaved or the best students in the class. Regardless of the group to which Kathy has categorized the boys, they command the teacher's attention through negative or positive means, and control the classroom.

Kathy's rendition of the life of her physics class is exactly what researchers report in many other coeducational classes. Male students are the dominant force in classrooms, receiving most of the teacher's attention. When Kathy leaves CA for physics class at the boys' school, she is moving from a place where she is of the dominant culture to one where she is not. Kathy struggles with a number of issues before she can begin to concentrate on learning the content. CA has imposed a tradeoff for Kathy and other upper school girls. She has the benefit of having the "good" teacher, but in the meantime, she must cross over into the culture of the boys' school where clearly she is uncomfortable.

Summary of Girls' Perceptions

Both Susan and Kathy believed they benefited from the single-sex context of CA. Susan's perceptions, at least in part, reflected her mother's beliefs about the importance of a girls-only structure, in connection with developmental issues of early adolescence and adolescence.

But Susan had constructed some of her own ideas, especially about a girls-only environment and her activities. The absence of boys allowed her to not "worry about her hair," and the presence of girls allowed her to "belong to all groups."

Kathy's perceptions were somewhat different. By virtue of spending much of her academic time in coeducational classrooms, and especially because she had to travel the footpath to the boys' school for science, she spoke of feelings that were clearly shaped by gender issues. Her sense of the physics teacher "clicking in" on the boys, and her detailed description of fearing the trip to the boys' school stand in clear contrast to the sense of relief she expresses when talking about returning to the safety of the halls and lounge of CA.

Susan looked forward to having coed classes, but Kathy, who was experiencing them, was struggling outside of the single-sex environment.

In returning to my original query about girls enrolled at a girls-only school, one point is clear: Being in classes with only girls holds benefits for them. This study found that they encountered fewer distractions to learning, they had all of the teacher's attention, and they did not need to make a space in a different culture. The culture was theirs, a place they understood and did not need to fear.

In the following chapter, we will hear the voices of girls in a variety of single-sex classes, all of which are in coeducational schools.

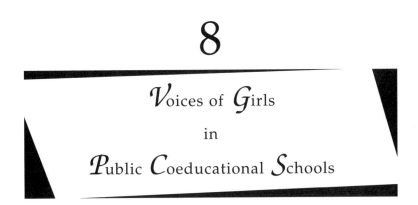

8

$\mathcal{V}$oices of $\mathcal{G}$irls

in

$\mathcal{P}$ublic $\mathcal{C}$oeducational $\mathcal{S}$chools

The other context in which single-sex schooling for girls can be studied is in girls-only classes in otherwise coeducational public schools. Much of this setting is quite different from a private, expensive girls' academy.

The girls in these coeducational schools represent a much greater span across the socioeconomic spectrum, provide a richer ethnic diversity, and have had no experience with either private or single-sex education prior to their experiences in the single-sex classes that they discuss here. The schools they attended during their enrollment in the single-sex classes were not only different from CA, but also different from each other.

Eastside Middle School, although located in a middle-class, predominantly European-descent neighborhood, has a fairly heterogeneous enrollment. The school was designated a math/science magnet school, enabling students from neighborhoods far from the school and students of non-European descent to transfer there. The school now has a cultural/ethnic composition that nearly matches that of the school district: approximately 52 percent European descent, 36 percent Latino/a, 5 percent African American, and 7 percent Native American and

Asian. The socioeconomic backgrounds of the students range from middle class to lower class.

Elgin High School is in a predominantly European-descent, middle- to lower-middle-class neighborhood. While it is a comprehensive high school, its primary curricular focus is on college preparation. The school administration reports that nearly 90 percent of the graduating class goes on to some form of higher education. The majority enroll in the local community college for their first year of college.

Williams High School is the oldest high school in the city. It is located in an urban neighborhood that is poor. Williams is a magnet high school with an emphasis on math, science, and fine arts. Although European-descent students from other areas of the district are free to transfer to Williams, its enrollment remains predominantly minority at 60 percent, compared to a 34 percent European-descent breakdown.

What began as a passing interest and a number of observations at these schools turned into a longitudinal study developed from interviews with girls in various single-sex settings (Appendix D) and their teachers. Several issues have emerged from this study from both classroom observations and interviews with the girls over the years. For example, virtually every girl who has been in one of these classes is glad to have had the opportunity. Further, many of them articulate what they consider to have been positive lasting effects from their girls-only experience, and often they reveal a sense of competence in math or science, which they credit with having been instilled in the girls-only class.

The first group of girls studied were, during 1992 through 1994, in a seventh through eighth grade math program in Eastside Middle School. During the 1996–97 school year, when follow-up interviews were conducted, they were juniors in high school. Those in the second group were in a girls-only physics class. The majority were in their second year of college during the 1996–97 year. The last group were in a cross-grade math class in high school and are now still in high school, have dropped out, or have finished high school. While each school setting is quite different from the others, the issues constructed by the girls were quite consistent across programs. Therefore, the data are reported as representative samples from the classes in the three schools.

The voices of the girls who were part of the girls-only classes during this study have resonated with several distinct themes that illustrate their perceptions of their experiences. But it is also important to explore some of the *differences* among the groups of girls, if not among them individually. For example, in observing their demeanor and talking with the girls during the actual time they were in the girls-only classes, it became obvious that their places in life varied developmentally, depending on whether they were in middle school or high school.

The middle school girls paid considerable attention to their appearance, applying makeup and combing their hair while they considered positive and negative numbers. The high school girls were quieter, more composed, and rarely, if ever, pulled out their grooming equipment during class. The high school girls were much less likely to giggle, whisper, or write notes, and their moods appeared to be more even than their middle school counterparts.

There appeared to be some very strong similarities between the two high school groups. This was despite the socioeconomic differences between Elgin and Williams high schools, and despite the differences in the level of the subject matter being taught. For example, the girls in the physics class at Elgin, most of whom one would expect to be college bound, and the girls in Williams' remedial math class, many of whom might be expected to finish high school at best, appeared to share the same level of aspiration for post-high school, and the same sense of what was important.

In the remedial math class, Cara identified "cruising, guys, partying, school, and both [playing and studying]" as important to her and her friends. A classmate, Angie, said: "The important thing I think is first to learn, but you have to have your friends to push you sometimes so that you can have confidence in yourself and go on." Chrissy identified "family and friends" as the most important thing. Ari thought "not getting pregnant" and "not dying like, since there are a lot of gangs. Taking care of our lives" were the critical issues.

When they thought about their somewhat less immediate futures and what they would like to do, the girls at Williams High talked about careers, just as the girls at Elgin High did. The Williams High girls listed lawyer, teacher, zoologist, and doctor as future career possibilities. Some were undecided. The Elgin girls talked about being a psychologist, astronaut, doctor, teacher, actress, and senator. Some of the girls at Elgin were undecided about their career goals too. The differences between the two groups of high school girls were there, shaded by socioeconomic issues. None of the Elgin High girls talked about being worried about dying violently or getting pregnant, and they described their futures more sharply. Their words describing their career goals were more sophisticated. For example, they talked about being pediatricians or psychiatrists rather than doctors. Some of their parents held those positions, and they were familiar with the work and the means to obtain the position. Some of the Williams High girls struggled with issues of safety and well-being that did not appear to be there for the Elgin High girls. Nonetheless, the Williams High girls looked beyond that and were beginning to think about ways to shape their future lives that were quite similar to the Elgin High girls. One Williams girl commented:

> Most of my friends and I care mostly about grades and going on to college. There are some girls in the school who care about boyfriends, but even my friends who do, still pay attention to doing well in school and thinking about going on to college. It isn't just getting married after high school.

When reflecting about the girls-only class experience, almost without exception, all of the girls who spoke did so similarly about their perceptions of themselves as learners of math or science, about the absence of boys in their class, and about the presence of girls.

The Girls as Learners

Whether the girls were in the all-girls class voluntarily, as was the case in the physics class at Elgin High, involuntarily, in the Williams High remedial math class, or one or the other in the middle school math program, the girls tended to feel that they were better students in the subject having been in the class and that they felt more confidence in their abilities because of the experience.

The physics students, while in the class, generally thought of themselves as good students and many of them talked about science as being one of their favorite subjects. All of the girls in the physics class talked about the importance of having a solid science background as they entered college. But when asked if they thought the girls-only context might contribute either positively or negatively to their sense of themselves as learners of science, among the girls interviewed, none felt the class was having a negative effect, three felt it made no difference, and the remainder believed it was beneficial.

Samantha's comments were representative of the girls who felt the girls-only venue was a neutral variable regarding attitudes toward achievement in science.

> I really like science, and I've always done well. There are a lot of things I like about this class, but no matter which class I took, I think I'd do well in physics.

Sunny's remarks are illustrative of those of the majority of girls interviewed. At the time of the initial interview, Sunny also talked about enjoying science:

> I like physics and I like science a lot. I'll probably major in it in college—either in math or science.

But she went on to describe the environment of a girls-only setting as one that directly affected her perceptions of herself and physics.

> I think this class makes me feel like girls can do science. I know the teacher told us after the first test that we [the

girls' class] had the best scores out of everyone [compared to the mixed-sex physics class]. That turns around the stereotype that girls are stupid and that we don't know anything about a science, 'cause in this society we feel like we don't know very much, but we do.

Amanda, beginning her second year as an art history major at a prestigious women's college in the Northeast, reflected on the girls-only physics experience and its possible effect on how she perceived herself as a scientist. Among the girls interviewed, only she described feelings of unease in the subject, despite the A she received in the course.

I never will feel confident about science. It will never be my strong point. It's just that part of my brain that's underdeveloped. I generally do well, but I'm not very comfortable with it. I'd rather write a paper about a painting than do a science lab.

The girls in the math class at Williams High were unanimous in their beliefs that the girls-only class had a positive effect on their attitudes toward math, with the exception of Toni. This belief was most often described as a strong sense of being successful. Ana's comparison of past and present experiences with math was echoed by the majority of girls interviewed. Ana explained:

I've always had problems with math. I've had problems since the third grade. And I was getting an F in my other class as usual. I went to my counselor and I said, "I'm so bad at math, I don't know what to do." He said, "There's this new thing going on where it's girls-only if you want to give it a shot."
I feel actually more independent in here. I feel like I can actually do it. Most of the time, the teachers were like, well, she can't do it. I would just always feel so stupid. But in here, everyone says, "You can do it." It makes me feel a lot better about myself and makes me know I'm not stupid.

Toni was the only student in the class who felt the absence of boys had a negative effect on her ability to learn math.

> Since I was small, I always liked math. I was always good in it. And then, I don't know what happened, I just . . . I was like in sixth grade and I like math but it changed for me.
>
> I've been in this course for two years. In this class it's different without the guys, 'cause you can talk to guys. They make it different. The guys seem more like they understand it. Well, the girls do too, but it's like the guys will help you more. I guess the girls expect you to know it already. And the guys are there to help you with it. I guess the guys expect that you won't know it.

Toni's sense of her ability in math was probably the lowest among the girls interviewed. She, more than any of the others, struggled throughout the school year to pass the class. Despite her reference to being able to talk with boys, and the following implication that she did not or could not work with girls, the observation data illustrated a situation quite to the contrary. She was, as were all the girls, at a table with three other girls, where most of the work was done collaboratively and with constant attention from one or both of the two teachers. There were no outward signs that her interactions with the other girls were any different than others in the class. Everyone worked together. It may be, in Toni's case, that her history of failure was so strongly entrenched, that no means of intervention would have had a positive effect on either her perceptions of her ability or her actual achievement. Perhaps her reference to needing boys, who she believed "do math better," was an effort to reach out to anything that she thought could rectify her failure.

The girls in the Eastside Middle School math program presented a pattern similar to the girls at Elgin High with regard to their previous achievement in the subject. Because the principal predicted these girls would do well in math during their seventh and eighth grade years, he hand-picked them as the participants for this program. Their pre-algebra class was the most accelerated course available to seventh graders at Eastside Middle and the girls entered the class with varying, but generally a high degree of, confidence of their abilities to do well.

Of the three groups, the Eastside Middle girls were the most enthusiastic about their experiences in the girls-only setting, both during and after the program. Kendall described how her confidence about—and willingness to display her competence in—math had been affected by her participation in the program.

> I consider myself a good student, but sometimes I've been afraid to show it. In here, it's okay to do well. I guess when I don't feel like I can answer questions in class and show people that I can do it, I start not liking the class and the things we're supposed to learn. But in here, I can be myself, feel smart, and get good grades. I'm going to take geometry next year in high school. I just wish that there were a girls-only class for that. But at least I feel like I can do the math. I know I can.

Another student, Nona, was not as confident of her ability at the beginning of the program. However, at the end of eighth grade, she said:

> Since this class, I've liked math a lot more than before. I see the usefulness of math in a lot of other things, like I'm into astronomy now, and you need math for that. If I had to start all over, I would take this class instead of the regular ones. There was still some stuff in it that I'm not sure I understood, so I'm going to take Algebra I next year in high school. And then I'll take geometry during the summer so I can catch up. That way I can be ready for calculus. I never thought I'd go on in math. In fact, a lot of my friends in the neighborhood talk about dropping out altogether. But I'm not going to do that, and I'm going to take more math. I do wish that there were more girls-only classes, some in high school. I feel better in them. I'm not afraid to ask questions and get things wrong. I'll miss being with just girls, but I think I'll be okay now.

Several years later, when this group of girls was in the tenth grade in various high schools throughout the city, a number of them reflected on their perceptions of the power of the girls-only setting, and how they believed its influence might be continuing to affect them as learners of math.

Karen began high school at a public 9–12 school for the gifted and talented. Admission is limited to about 600 students who must pass an entrance exam, produce high achievement test scores, have a high grade-point average from middle school, and have teacher recommendations. The school annually produces the highest number of National Merit Scholars in the city, and students go on to nearly any colleges of their choice. Nearly 100 percent of the senior class goes on to a four-year college or university each year. Toward the end of the tenth grade, Karen decided to transfer to a comprehensive high school, saying that she found the climate at her previous school too competitive and intense. Despite her apparent discomfort at College High, she had received As and Bs in Honors Algebra and geometry and intended to continue with trigonometry during her junior year. As Karen thought back to the girls-only classes, she focused on the issue of the climate of the class that she believed enhanced her ability to learn.

> Now I'm in math class, and I don't ask as many questions as I did with the girls-only. I never ask a question a second time even when I still don't get it, because I'd just look dumb. The class with Ms. Mary [girls-only class at Eastside Middle School] was so open that I would have said, "Hey, I still don't understand it. Do it one more time." But now I don't want anyone to think there's something wrong with me. And of course, there's always the intimidation of being made fun of. I don't speak up. The girls-only math class was a great experience and it helped me think in math. Yeah, I grew to like math a lot. I think I'm even going to go to college to be a math teacher. I still see Ms. Mary sometimes, and she said maybe I could end up getting a job at the high school where she teaches now.

Even though Karen was struggling with her ability to be assertive in her current math classes, she remembered the girls-only math class as being an experience that had built up her sense of self as a mathematician. The class, as well as the teacher, had contributed in a powerful way to shaping how she saw her future at that point in time. Despite her fears and struggles in her current math class, she was persevering in her aspirations that were connected with math.

After middle school, Jenny also entered College High. Unlike Karen, she liked the school and was going to remain there throughout high school. She and Karen had been in the same math classes during their first and second years of high school. Jenny had done well in algebra but not so well in geometry. Instead of going on to trigonometry as a junior, she planned on taking Algebra II. She was unsure of what she wanted to study in college but was clear that math would not be central in her studies. Jenny remembered the girls-only math program as one where she did well and felt confident about her math abilities.

> I liked math more in Ms. Mary's class and I felt more confident. It seems like each year that I get further away from that class I feel less comfortable in asking questions when I don't understand. If I could take another all-girls class, it would definitely be a math class. Math is my hardest subject and I think that in my hardest subject if I was surrounded by my friends, you know, girls, I would feel more comfortable.

Nora was a third student in the study who entered College High. She too expected to stay until graduation and planned to take Honors Pre-calculus/Trigonometry as a junior. When thinking back to the girls-only program, she said:

> I remember being able to express yourself. It's easier to express yourself when it's just a room with all girls as compared to coed. I liked it better. In my math class now, one of my former colleagues from the all-girls class and I

sit there and we wish we were in another all-girls class. I don't like this. It's [girls-only classes] easier. You don't feel as much pressure if it's all girls. Generally I'm not a math/science person and the whole experience with Ms. Mary helped me give myself more patience and give it [math] more time.

Class without Boys

A second theme that emerged for all of the girls was life in a classroom without boys. Because the girls-only classes in otherwise coeducational public schools were developed expressly as girls-only, this appears to be a rather obvious issue that the students would want to talk about. Furthermore, this was a point about which there was little difference in opinion among all of the girls. In general, they talked about middle school and high school boys as distracting and often annoying. The idea that, without boys, the girls could and did get their work done resonated throughout each interview. Among the Elgin High girls were some of the following comments when they were asked about being in a class without boys:

I do like that there are no guys in here. And I think it's because in my other classes with guys that they're obnoxious. They tend to be more distracting. With all girls in here, it's more relaxing. I like it. (Andi)

In my chemistry class last year, it was the girls who got the work done and the guys squirted water. In all my other science classes it's been the girls who try to get the work done. Without guys it's not so distracting. (Amanda)

It seems like girls can work and talk at the same time. But when it's males and females, you tend to give them [males] all of your attention. (Sunny)

As sophomores in college, Amanda and Sunny had several points to make both in reflection about what it had been like without boys in their physics class, as well as what current experiences they were encountering. Amanda's classes at the prestigious Northeast college were almost always single-sex and she clearly had developed expectations as to what that would mean with regard to the behavior of the women at the college.

> Something surprising happened. We had some like race relation problems. . . . I was really surprised and I thought with women, people would be able to work it out better, cause you know, whenever I think of women I assume that they're more sensible or calm about this sort of thing. But we had a couple of protests during the year, because they wanted to add a Middle Eastern Studies Department or a Far Eastern Studies Department or something. The college wouldn't do it, so there was this huge heated debate with screaming and shouting and prank phone calls and nasty e-mails. That was really surprising. I thought . . . these women should be above it. And it seemed like such a "boy" thing to do. It seemed immature to me. But that was the only thing this year that I thought, "Why is this happening at a school full of women?" Maybe it's because there aren't enough women role models for women to follow when they want to protest something.

Sunny was in her second year at the largest of three state universities in her home state. She decided on a civil engineering major early in her first year. She was happy with her choice and confident that she would continue with it. Several things concerned her, though, chief among them was the fact that there were so few women in the major. When asked how she felt this was affecting her, she explained that she wished it were more balanced with regard to gender, and went on to relate this story:

> I'm planning to take Calculus III, physics and another engineering class. I'm feeling very confident in math and science. But something happened in one of my classes. Most of my classes are almost all guys. For this one lab, we were put into groups. There were three guys, me and another girl. It always happened that we would do the

writing. When we had to work on things in class, whatever, we [the other girl and Sunny] would do the secre-
tarial work, the organizing, the holding of papers. And I
didn't even realize this until maybe like halfway through
and then I said, "Hey, I'm not doing it may more." And I
gave it to one of the guys, and they wouldn't do it. It was
just weird to me how they refused to write anything
down. It was stuck between the other girl and me for the
whole semester. They were really difficult to deal with. It
came to the point where they were making sexist jokes
all the time and you know, ha, real funny.

In retrospect, I liked the physics class at Eastside. I
liked the camaraderie. You just felt more comfortable. I
just liked the equal level.

With the exception of one student, those in an all-girls class
at Williams High concurred about the effect of boys on their
behavior in their other classes.

I have found it a lot easier to kick back and be myself. In
other classes, it's like, if I act like myself, guys just look at
me like you are such an idiot. In most of my classes they
[boys] talk and they expect me to sit back and talk with
them. And what am I supposed to say—"Oh, no I have to
finish this work?" It's "No, don't work, have fun." (Ana)

I think that I can probably concentrate more in this class
because boys, like they're very loud and all the screaming, so I look over there to see what they're screaming
about and I lose my concentration to what I was doing.
It's easier here than it is with the guys in the class. And
you don't want to be wrong, because then they'll probably
say something that will make you feel stupid. (Angie)

With boys, you're embarrassed. If you say something
wrong the guys are going to laugh at you. And they're
going to make fun of you. Here they don't. The girls in
here help you, not make fun of you. (Ari)

The same theme, and nearly the same words, prevailed
with the girls at Eastside Middle.

It's real different. It's easier to learn when you can just turn around, and you don't have to worry that there's this boy who's going to turn around and say, "You don't know that?" You can just turn around to the girl in back of you and say, "What do you mean by this?" Or if you find someone [a girl] who has the same problem, it's just different from finding some guy who has the same problem. (Terri)

It's better with just girls in the math class. There aren't any guys. So . . . if you mess up on a problem, they [boys] won't just sit there and laugh at you because it's all girls. (Andrea)

Yesterday I got a paper back in my language arts class. Nobody really wanted to show each other their grades if they did bad. But it's different in this class. Nobody really cares. Someone will just say, "Everybody makes mistakes sometimes." But in those other classes, a boy will say, "You got an F? Wow, you must be stupid or something!" In this class, it's just like, "Well, ya know. The test was hard." And there's usually somebody else who got the same grade as you for the same reason. (Kendall)

In my other classes, if someone makes a mistake, other people see something that they think is not right. And it's not really that, but they'll go around and spread it around, and they don't really care if anybody gets hurt. Girls and guys do that in mixed classes, but in this class none of the girls do that. I think we feel special together, and nobody would do that in here, even if they might in another class. We work together. (Jessie)

Class with Girls

This last statement by Jessie points not only to how she felt about not having boys in the class, but it also suggests what turned out to be a third theme developed by the girls in each of the classes. Even the several girls who were ambivalent about not having boys in the class described their sense of what it was like to have a community of girls in their class. Some of the girls at Elgin High said this about being with girls:

> All of the girls relate to each other pretty much. It's neat. (Andi)

From her perspective as a college sophomore at the Northeast college, Amanda described her memories of her first all-female educational experience:

> I think that class had a major helping hand in helping me decide to go to [a women's college]. I think being in that class—we had so much fun and it made it easier to imagine the idea of having only women in classes from there on out. I learned how to learn with other women. Some of it was social, but that was an important part too. And I definitely learned better.

Randi was a physical therapy major in her sophomore year at the largest university in the state. Throughout each of the interviews with her over the three years, she stressed the importance of the issue of being in classes with "other smart people." She still harbored this point as critical, but she also wove in what it was like with "smart girls."

> Well, my friends were in that class, and there were other smart girls in there I hadn't known before. It was kind of neat because a lot of times in my other science classes there were a lot of slower people and so this was great having a lot of smart girls to be with. The other thing was, in this class, the smart girls could show they were smart. And we could all work together and that made it really special.

The Williams High girls felt similarly about having just themselves in their class.

> I like that you can work, that you work in groups and that everybody tries to work together and help each other out. And they're not criticizing. The girls will just

kid with you, and so you try to do it again and it's easier. (Angie)

I've made a lot of new friends in the class. All the girls are my friends. They've helped me and now I'm passing. If I have a problem, there are a lot of girls there who understand, 'cause they go through the same thing. (Ari)

The middle school girls expressed parallel views about the idea that being with just girls was a very special thing that transcended the issue of having a class without boys. Kris described her feelings:

I'm so glad to have had the experience of being in an all-girls class. To understand that that's possible, that type of teaching environment is possible. Guys don't have to be in all-guys classes to succeed I don't think, because they have no problem succeeding in a mixed-gender class. But girls have a much better chance of learning, understanding, having a chance to speak up and give their ideas if it's all girls. It has a lot to do with self-esteem. With guys in the class, they don't make it very easy for people [girls] to develop that esteem, to be able to stand up and say anything. If I had to choose whether to have a girls-only experience early or later in school I'd have to say to have it later on. That's how you could finish learning the more complicated stuff, or that's how you could refine the stuff you learned earlier on. It's just a different situation—more nurturing.

Kris's idea about saving the girls-only experience for the end of schooling is opposite to the approach taken by Connecticut Academy for example. But it is exactly the route that Amanda decided to take when she entered the Northeast women's college. The philosophy of Connecticut Academy is that while a single-sex experience is powerful and important to learning, some integration by gender is critical, not only to ensure that the girls experience a greater variety of instructors by going to the boys' school for classes, but also to provide them with a mixed-gender, or real-world situation before entering college. On the other hand, Kris and Amanda—perhaps because they did not have the opportunity to attend a single-sex school earlier in their schooling—believe that saving it for later would be more beneficial, almost as if the experience were the dessert of their schooling.

Summary of Girls' Perceptions

All of the girls interviewed—both during and after their girls-only schooling experiences—spoke of similar issues. Not only was there almost total consensus that the classes had been beneficial in an academic sense, but they expressed the belief that without boys and with girls, their learning was heightened. Without the boys, they were more focused on the content. But there was more in these classrooms than simply getting the work done. There was ease and they had camaraderie. The girls-only settings, whether at Connecticut Academy or in the public coeducational schools, allowed the girls the opportunity to set aside their need to struggle for attention from the teacher and control of the classroom. The girls were the only ones to be called on, they asked and answered questions without the risk of "feeling stupid," and felt more empowered for it. As Kendall said:

> In a mixed class, you can probably learn almost as much, but you're like off in the background. I know that it should be up to you as a person to decide whether you want to be in the front of things or in the background, but in this class I guess it's easier to make that choice. In the other classes, you're quieter about what you know—about asking questions and stuff. You just don't participate in it as much. I definitely learn more this way. I'm still not that much in the front in my other classes, but now I feel like I could be if I wanted to.

9

*T*aking a *S*tep
beyond
*T*itle *IX*

In her book *The Difference* (1996), Judy Mann describes
what she considers to be differences—culturally imposed
and/or inherent—between girls and boys. She takes up
the unpopular position that we must reshape our thinking
about gender differences and similarities before we can devise
solutions to some of the longstanding gender issues that seem
to face us in schools and other elements of the broader culture.
Women can achieve equality and we can reconsider how to
empower them only if we can step aside from the feminist construct that says females must be considered *like* males.

Agreeing that this is so, or even agreeing that it *may* be so,
is a giant step apart from what has stood as liberal feminist,
political dogma since the 1970s. Further, the construct that
women must be considered the same as men in order to maintain or gain ground in the struggle for equality, is that upon
which federal policy, most local practice, and court decisions
affecting females in schools are based. Consideration of differences, which in turn could be used as the bases of an argument
for more or different resources, is ignored or denied. Yet there
seems to be more than sufficient evidence that tells us there
are gender differences. The historical as well as current cul-

ture in schools renders females as a group at risk, and current practice rarely creates adequate changes to ensure that, as a group, female students will have the same quality and quantity of schooling experiences as male students.

As chronicled in chapter 3, the historical picture of women's schooling in this country depicts both schools and curriculum as differentiated from that of men's. The expectation for girls, when schooled, was that they would assume very specific roles within society, and the quality and quantity of their schooling was designed to prepare them for those roles.

Even with the predominance of coeducation by the beginning of the twentieth century, some differentiation remained, particularly in curricula and certainly with regard to career expectations. The curricular differences may best be remembered by many of us in the guise of sewing and cooking classes versus drafting, auto mechanics, and woodworking classes. The more subtle curricular differences concerning issues such as girls' participation and achievement in upper-level math and science courses continued and remains a contemporary issue.

As we look back at the historical situation, one point is clear: Although women's options were extremely limited, there was alignment between the schools and their curriculum. Today, however, with unlimited options available to women, there is a dysjuncture between schooling and expectations. In theory, females participate equally with males. Title IX decrees and generally enforces equal access, but what has not followed is the opportunity for equal educational experiences. Coeducational, public schools continue to be places where young women not only feel disenfranchised, but, in reality, are.

Research in coeducational classrooms shows repeatedly that female students receive less opportunity quantitatively and qualitatively than male students. Although the grades of females tend to be better, males continue to score better than females on most standardized tests, especially in math and science (U.S. Department of Education 1996). While the gender gap in math achievement has narrowed over the past several decades, 1996 statistics indicate that the gap, while stable, continues to exist. At the same time, the gender difference in science standardized scores is increasing.

School culture, in general, is male-oriented. Male students receive far more positive as well as negative attention from adults in schools. Boys dominate the classrooms, and their achievements tend to be the ones celebrated, especially in connection with sports. Their voices are heard loudly, while the voices of the female students are, as a group, only a murmur. Also, girls are far less safe in our schools than boys. While violent acts claim more young men than women in the streets, acts of harassment and abuse in school hallways and classrooms are most often directed at girls in school (Bailey 1992).

Finally, issues of declining self-esteem, beginning in middle school, while important for boys, are critical for girls. The evidence, in other words, points to the fact that public, coeducational schools continue to not be "user-friendly" places for female students.

The research on single-sex school settings, most of which is quantitative, does not provide conclusive findings that mixed-sex groupings are more beneficial than single-sex groupings. Results of achievement tests and measures that examine more affective issues suggest that in some cases single-sex groupings appear to enhance scores for one gender and/or the other. Still, there is, as yet, no perfectly clear indicator as to whether these groupings might in and of themselves be a causal factor.

This is the case with single-sex classes and programs in coeducational schools in England and Australia, where single-sex settings have been in place for some time. It's also the case in the research on single-sex schools in the United States. But it seems as if quantitative measures are able to tell only part of the story. What is missing from this literature is a truer and more personal sense of the girls themselves.

The study detailed here provides us with a clearer picture of how girls in girls-only settings feel, what they believe, and what they want, rather than simply what their test scores are. The girls in all of the girls-only classes talked about their sense of being focused as learners, being in control of the classroom, and being able to take risks. These sentiments were expressed both within the context of not being with boys, and of being with only girls. The absence of boys lessens the distractions, both for the girls and for the teacher. But more importantly, being with only girls allows girls to create their own space, their own culture.

The girls-only classrooms become places where the girls feel valued as they are. This was expressed by the girls in the most concrete way, such as they didn't need to worry about their makeup or hair. It also was described in more subtle ways, such as in the conversations with Ari and Angie at Williams High, who said that the girls helped each other out, and furthermore, they behaved in more caring and considerate ways toward one another within the girls-only context than in their mixed-gender classes.

The question of how well the girls did academically in the girls-only classes at Eastside, Elgin, and Williams is not *unimportant,* but it is impossible to construct the academic achievement of these girls as a definitive indication that a girls-only class is *better* than a mixed-sex class. Within the four classes at Eastside, there was a wide range of grades. In a few cases, girls failed the class. In a number of cases, they received As. In the physics class at Elgin, the number of As far outstripped the As awarded in the mixed-sex class, and in the math class at Williams two of the girls failed, one dropped out of school, and the remainder passed the class. What is impossible to know, of course, is whether in a mixed-sex class these individual girls would have achieved more, less, or at the same level as in the girls-only class.

What we do know, with regard to the subject matter they studied, is that in having had the girls-only class experience, nearly all of the girls expressed a sense of feeling better about themselves in the subjects of math and science. Research in the area of attitude about oneself in connection with a particular subject matter (e.g., Fox, Brody, and Tobin 1980; Sherman 1980) indicates that there is a strong link between students' confidence levels and their achievement. The girls' positive attitudes about themselves as math or science learners then suggests that their achievement in the girls-only classes may have been enhanced beyond what it would have been in a mixed-sex class.

There is, of course, always a reluctance to credit young people with knowing what is good for them. But the beliefs of the adults connected with the single-sex settings were just as strongly stated and as strongly supportive of the power of these classes as those of the girls. Even given the wide range of general teaching expertise, training in and commitment to gender-equity issues, the belief in the power of the context of girls-only classes was unvarying among the teachers and administrators interviewed.

From Mr. Paul, who has spent his professional life teaching at Connecticut Academy, and Ms. Mary, who moved from skepticism to zealousness, to Mr. Gordon, who believed in the principles of military hierarchy and patriarchy, the teachers considered their girls-only classes to be places where their students could *do* more and where a foundation might be laid so that the girls could ultimately *be* more.

Views of Pre-Service Teachers

As this study progressed, one of the more intriguing themes that emerged from the conversations with the girls-only teachers in the public schools was that the teachers tended to have only their own experiences and perceptions about gender issues to guide them in their girls-only classes. Some feminist teachers and teachers of feminism, in the field of teacher education and other fields, agree that teaching about issues of gender, however constructed, is difficult.

My own experience of nearly twenty years of working with prospective teachers in teacher education programs has taught me that it is the rare student, female or male, who is willing to confront her or his own bias or even to accept the notion that gender-equity issues remain in our schools. The students with whom I have worked tend to consider that "the problem" has been addressed, largely because Title IX has mandated that sex discrimination will not be tolerated. The fact that public policy exists seems to satisfy most of the students with whom I have come in contact. If the federal government has decreed that gender inequities are not allowable, then certainly these inequities no longer exist.

I also have found that many of the younger students, for whom the Civil Rights movement and the work for passage of the Equal Rights Amendment are ancient history, believe that my generation, and those preceding mine, fought the fight, won the war, and that there are no more gender issues to be addressed. Gender inequities they observe in classrooms are anomalies and are not based on issues far more complex, broadly constructed, and systemic within the larger culture. Somehow they have come to believe that due to the existence of federal policy, they need not concern themselves with their own beliefs or actions in the classrooms as they teach both boys and girls.

While the purpose of this study was not directly connected with the substance of teacher education programs, we did ask several teacher education students about their views of gender-equity issues in teaching, in general, and what they thought of the idea of girls-only classes, specifically in public, coeducational schools.

In the broadest sense, these students seemed to represent the newest wave of teachers. I was interested in the views of prospective teachers about gender issues in their teaching. Would the students, all entering school after Title IX began, report their schooling experiences as having been gender equitable? What would be their response to the concept of girls-only classes? While the responses of the interviewed students can in no way be construed as representative of teacher education students in general, themes emerged from their comments that were quite distinct by gender.

Four students, all in the first semester of their initial teacher education program, were interviewed. The two women and two men were in their early twenties, the two men were of European descent as was one of the women, and the other woman was African American. They represented a variety of majors. Chet was a music education major, and Ted was a science major and math minor. Melissa, the African American, was an elementary education major, and Leslie was a science major.

When asked about their general thoughts connected with gender equity in schools, Ted and Chet both commented that they had not noticed any inequities, but if any were to occur, they were certain that they would notice them. Ted commented:

Well, I've sort of heard about gender equity in teaching. But as far as I've ever noticed in the classrooms I've observed and worked in, things were all kind of equal. [If I were shown a film, or observed in a class] where gender bias was going on, I'd be able to identify it. And if I was the one doing it, I'd notice it. But, other than seeing the usual adolescent hormones raging, like the guys just sort of being loud, because that's in any high school classroom that you go into, I think things are pretty equal.

Chet was even less concerned:

When thinking about gender equity in classes, I'd probably say that it would be okay and not think anything of it.

The men were asked to remember any times during their own school experiences when they believed that gender issues may have occurred. Chet recalled some incidents:

There were a couple of times in gym class, not like in science or math classes, when the guys were a little out of hand. The guys would be talking about the girls in front of them, making rude comments. [The reaction of the girls] was mixed. Some of them would laugh at us, some would get pretty offended. But that didn't stop anybody.

Ted applied the question to his teachers:

In high school, everybody was pretty much on the same level. I don't remember any groups of students. And I didn't notice any different levels of achievement between the girls and the boys. But I do think there were differences between the men and women teachers.

The female teachers usually tended to be more available outside of class, whereas the male teachers usually were working on research or projects. But then again, the male teachers were often more involved in the clubs.

Both men were asked to think about the idea of girls-only classes as a possibility in coeducational schools. Chet said: "It wouldn't matter to me. I wouldn't think anything of it."

Ted disagreed with any form of segregation: "To tell you the truth, I don't really agree with segregation in any aspect."

Compared to the men, the two women responded in very different ways to these questions. The women appeared to be more attentive to gender issues and to have more distinct memories about their own experiences. Their reactions to girls-only classes were distinct as well. Melissa said:

> We've talked a lot about gender issues in most of my education classes, along with teacher expectations. How to think about "wait time" with girls, how to be more sensitive. And it always surprises me because I think that we [women] are [more sensitive]. We learn about it all, being women.

Leslie too said it was a familiar topic: "Yes, we've talked about teaching and gender. It's something that comes up in most of my classes."

Both women had sharp recollections about their own experiences that were gender-related.

Melissa recalled:

> The gender competition was always there. It was just the way I reacted to it. There was a lot of it [gender bias] in my schools. I was real expressive, and I think that a lot of my teachers shoved me to the side because I wasn't a girl to lead. I didn't get mouthy until I got in high school, but even there it was still unacceptable. I was rather shy in elementary and middle school. I was so nice, but when I wanted to play basketball and I liked football, it was like . . . hard to be accepted doing that. I remember that it was totally unacceptable for me to argue.
>
> For instance, I got into an argument my sophomore year in high school with this one guy who I guess couldn't stand the fact that I was always expressing dissent when they were talking about discrimination or anything. And

he just did not like that and started making racial slurs and girl slurs. I was walking by and he spit on me. Of course, I was irate. I was appalled that someone would spit on me. What ended up happening was that he hit me, and I pushed him back after he hit me. I just couldn't take it any more—trying to be non-violent.

Then I went to the principal's office, and I remember how disappointed I was because the principal thought that if I was such a great student but why was I fighting this boy? He never asked him what in the world would make him want to hit a girl. It really disappointed me that he would be disappointed in me because it was not ladylike.

Leslie recalled less extreme experiences:

When I was in school, I saw a lot of my girlfriends who would have benefited from better gender equity. In my case, I don't think it was, because I tended to do just fine in math and science classes, surrounded by boys.

I don't think personally I had any trouble. But I think a lot of girls feel intimidated especially in math and science classes. I think it happens more there, in terms of raising their hand, asking questions.

I think there were friends of mine who were not particularly less talented than anybody else, but they never made an effort in the class [math/science]—speaking out, finding out more about the subject, because they felt intimidated by the boys who did often dominate. And I think a lot of it personally has to do with each girl. If they want to be a good science or math student they need to overcome some sort of—what do you call it, discrimination, that starts early on. I may have been lucky in the sense that I had teachers who never said, "You're a girl. You can't do that." Until I got to college, of course.

Melissa and Leslie also commented about the idea of girls-only classes. In Leslie's case, she had been a student of Mr. James two years before the creation of his girls-only physics class. She not only found the girls-only class an interesting concept, she also had the opportunity to talk with those who were in the class about her own aspirations as a physics major. She related that experience:

> I had a chance to talk with the girls, and they asked me all kinds of questions. I told them I was a really stubborn person, so when faced with someone who told me I couldn't do this [get a degree in physics], and made to feel it was just because I was a girl, I just said, "You've got to ignore those people." Another thing about that class, Mr. James brought in a woman scientist. People still think about scientists or physicists or astronomers as a man. There's something like 90 percent of the professors in astronomy and physics who are male. That's just a fact, so that's what they're seeing. But I think that a lot of the women should be doing more in terms of going to classes and saying "Women can do this." That's one thing I liked about that [girls-only] class. The girls got a chance to see what you can do and not get discouraged. It's a reaffirming kind of thing. Maybe the girls in that class had a seed in the back of their head that said they could do it before, but now they actually see, "Yeah, I can."

Melissa seemed to be trying to understand a need for sex segregation and conceded that it might be okay in some cases:

> I think [whether a girls-only class is a good idea or not] depends on the objectives of the class. I don't know that I would send my child to an all-boys or -girls school, but this idea is different. I guess what they're trying to do here is create a level playing field. I don't think it would be a negative thing. It's worth a try.

In the interview, I had been interested in Leslie's earlier comment, "Until I got to college, of course," so I was eager to hear her thoughts now that she's into higher education. In her reflections about her experiences in classes both in high school, as well as at the university, she described her sense of sexism as a parallel issue with racism.

Here at the university, I find that there are boys who don't want girls in their study groups because they think girls can't possibly be smart enough. I have had experiences in classes where guys would basically discredit any girl's comments. There were three or four in all of my classes, in a thirty-person class, and they [males] would discount what we [women] said. Often times it's better not to bring up the fact that as a woman you're being treated badly, like being made into the secretary of the group. It's just going to make a big discussion where the guys are going to deny holding any resentment for the girls being in their classrooms. I mean, nobody's going to admit that, because it's like being a racist. They're not going to say "Yeah, well I don't think you're smart enough because you're a woman." So rather than making everybody uncomfortable, oftentimes you just have to maybe stomach it a little. Most of the time it doesn't hurt me, it hurts them more because they're not able to really understand other people.

I've experienced these problems with gender issues and sexism. So when I become a teacher, I'll pay attention to this. You can ignore it, and hope everything gets better, which it doesn't. That's not what we want. Maybe I just got lucky and didn't get too discouraged about being in science. But I can see how many girls aren't that lucky. This [girls-only classes] might be one way to approach dealing with the sexism.

The comments of these teacher education students raise several issues. First and most striking is the difference by sex in the qualitative nature of the responses. The two men had few memories of gender issues in their own schooling. Further, neither believed that gender equity was a substantive issue in teaching today. In fact, neither identified it as a topic that had received much attention in any of their teacher education classes. To them, gender was a non-issue.

In sharp contrast, the women had immediately recalled memories of their own experiences of being girls in schools where they confronted gender issues. Their memories were not pleasant ones, and their voices were tinged with pain and frustration. In Leslie's case, there was considerable denial about her own feelings with regard to gender bias. "Some of her friends" and "other girls" had been through a number of difficult times being girls in a boys' culture. Leslie's detailed accounts of what her "friends" had felt and experienced were so personal in nature, that one can't help but believe that she had encountered the same experiences, but wasn't yet ready to think about what the experiences meant for her as a woman, although she was prepared to think about them in the context of being a teacher.

Clearly, from these interviews with four prospective teachers, the women recognized that gender issues were ones brought forward in their teacher education classes, and the men had only the vaguest notions that this topic had been addressed at all. The recognition that gender is an issue of oppression was not obvious to the two men. Melissa believed the women "got it because we're women." Personal experience played a role in the ability of these two women to understand that their gender had been a major factor in shaping their lives.

The point here is not necessarily about a greater need in teacher education programs for systematically addressing gender issues in teaching, although certainly the need is there. Instead, the concern is about how the continuing inequitable environment of schools can be reconstructed. After talking with Chet and Ted, I held out no hope for any gender issues being addressed in their own classrooms. However, the residual effect from talking with Melissa and Leslie was worse for me. The two women expressed anger, denial, and frustration about their past and current gendered experiences. There also was resignation in their voices. They each understood the risks in not being "ladylike" or in asserting their point of view. It seemed that they both had developed a persona so they could "get along" and not stand out within the traditional school culture.

I have come to think of Melissa and Leslie as representing both the positive and negative aspects of Title IX. As an African American woman, Melissa has benefited from desegregation mandates grounded in the principle of equality. She has attended racially/culturally desegregated schools and has been granted access to all areas of her schools' curricular offerings. Leslie has pursued her dream of becoming a science teacher. She has had access to upper-level science courses and has succeeded academically in them. What is missing from their memories of their schooling experiences is a sense of achievement "because of . . . ." Instead they talked about "learning lessons" and "overcoming." Melissa and Leslie may have achieved "in spite of . . . ."

Policy as Affirmative Action and/or Reparation

The primary argument against girls-only classrooms appears to center on the concern that any setting that is separate is inherently unequal, and therefore not beneficial for the group set apart from the mainstream. In her faxed statement to the author, Conners (1997) of the New York chapter of NOW, refer to the Young Women's Leadership Academy as representing an "illusion" of a remedy. She said: "Proponents of the school have argued that it is a form of affirmative action for girls. We reject this argument: Affirmative action has always been about inclusion, not about segregation."

Indeed, affirmative action has often been about inclusion, but it also has been about reparation. The principle behind all affirmative action has been the notion that individuals representing certain groups historically and systematically have been denied visibility and voice within the dominant culture. Girls-only settings are about affirmative action, and they are also about reparation.

Under the framework of equality, goals for equal hiring and admission have been created as a means for rectifying that injustice. In the case of gender equity, Title IX has provided an essential first step in the process of societal awareness of long-standing issues of gender inequities. But equal access has not been sufficient, and the creation of girls-only groupings represents another attempt at providing reparation, especially in light of the evidence that policies and practices framed by the principle of equality, have not provided sufficient remedy to the problems encountered by female students in public, coed-ucational schools.

Gender Equity, Not Equality

Gender equity practices nearly always are iterated according to the principles and framework of equality. Equality in prac-tice relies on the point of equal access to resources. Belief in this form of affirmative action, as Conners would have it, requires us to assume that once admitted to the school, pro-gram, or class, women will, as a group, have the same quality of opportunity and experience as men. On an individual or case-by-case basis, women will benefit differently among themselves, but the principle implies that there will be no out-comes differentiated by sex.

In other words, academic test scores and career aspirations and attainment will not be discernible by sex, nor will more *affective* measures such as self-esteem be sex-specific (Strom-quist 1993). Clearly, current evidence in all of these areas sug-gests that this approach has not been sufficient.

The theoretical framework of equity provides a broader per-spective on how an approach to gender equity might be con-strued and presents principles upon which the construction of girls-only settings are based. This framework allows for a larger frame of reference when considering what constitutes a more powerful means of affirmative action and reparation for female students.

The term *equity* in reference to *gender* equity has increas-ingly been used to mean "treatment that is fair to women both in form and result" (Jacklin 1981, 56). Jacklin's discussion of the derivation of the term suggests how it can be applied to girls-only groupings in schools:

Equity is a particular type of Anglo-Saxon justice that developed separately from the English common law. The common law provided the fundamental basis for Ameri-can jurisprudence and rests on the premise that the duty of the courts is to apply rules of law or precedents established in earlier cases. Historically, the common law courts are hostile to change, including legislative change. In contrast, equity jurisprudence raised fairness above the application of strict rules of precedent. The development of equity permitted the application of mitigating principles to cases where the result under the common law would be unfair, thereby defeating substantial justice. Because equity placed fairness above traditional rules of law, the concept of equity is an appropriate intellectual construct for feminists who aim to improve the legal status of women and claim that our legal system has served as a vehicle of women's subjection. (P. 56)

The concept of equity as the basis for remedy of gender inequities in schools suggests that what is fair is not necessarily equal. Simply removing barriers of access to females does not address the issues of inequitable treatment once they are admitted, nor does it constitute a means of restructuring the existing culture of schools and classrooms, which would be required in order to make schools truly inclusive. Public coeducational schools are Euro-male centric cultures, and until this is no longer the case, females as a group represent a subculture and continue to be marginalized.

In her article, "Interrupting Patriarchy: Politics, Resistance, and Transformation in the Feminist Classroom" (1990), Magda Lewis writes of her own experiences and those of her students within the context of what she describes as a "feminist classroom." Her article is dedicated to the fourteen women who were massacred at the Universite de Montreal on December 6, 1989, by a man who acted out the most extreme measure against women he identified as "you bunch of feminists" (p. 468). Lewis's (1990) work considers how to create classroom environments where women can come to understand themselves as women, apart from the mainstream patriarchal culture. To be sure, there are sharp differences between the description of Lewis's classroom and those described here as examples of girls-only classrooms. Nonetheless, there are important themes developed from Lewis's experiences that speak to the creation of girls-only settings.

Lewis shapes her classroom according to feminist structures. In establishing the framework for her own beliefs, she refers to Pierson's (1987, 203) definition of *feminism,* in which one characteristic of feminism is identified as the pursuit of autonomy for women. In this pursuit, there's a keen awareness of a sex/gender system on which society is organized, which provides power and autonomy to men and relegates women to dependence and subordination. Feminists insist that women and women's experiences are important, but to become a feminist perspective in this sex/gender system, a woman-centered perspective must be politicized by the experience of women in conflict with male dominance (in Lewis 1990, 470).

According to this definition, none of the girls-only classrooms described in this study constitutes a feminist setting, at least based solely on their organization. Simply putting young women together in a classroom does not a feminist classroom make. And if the definition of a feminist classroom is dependent in part on feminist intent of the teacher, many of these classroom settings fall short.

In the most extreme example, Mr. Gordon's intent was to construct a classroom full of girls who would follow the rules and be entirely controlled by him. His idea of a "good" classroom was one that was characterized by militaristic procedure and conformed to an extremely patriarchal structure.

Yet, in each of the classrooms, regardless of the teacher's intent, despite the lack of intentional feminist ideologies or pedagogies, the girls constructed places/cultures where they began to think about themselves as females within a male culture. Two members of the girls-only math program at Eastside Middle School described their sense of this during interviews a year following their two-year experience in the single-sex program. Chris said:

> [The class] was really unique. It was a bonding situation. It was a place where you could go and learn and just relax. It's kind of odd when I think about it, but I guess you [girls] are kind of uptight in most of your classes. I get really jumpy. In that class, I felt accepted. It was like

I belonged. It wasn't just that I felt I could ask questions without worrying about some boy calling me stupid. It was things like talking with the other girls about things that matter to me. It was a place where I understood everything that was going on.

Naomi also expressed the importance of "feeling a part" or "belonging":

In my mixed math class this year, everything is different. People are hyper and talking, and the guys are always talking about their sports. And the teacher is into that too. He's not a coach, but he talks about their [boys'] sports with them during class. I'm not part of that [boys' sports] and I just want to do the math. It's funny, but when I think about it, last year in the girls' class, we talked all the time. It was probably as noisy in there as it is this year. But I was part of it then, and altogether we did our math and talked too. This year, I don't talk and it's hard to do the math.

Their words echo a recurrent theme expressed by the girls in each of the girls-only classes, and their reflections, at age fourteen, are remarkably similar to those of an adult woman student in Lewis's class, who said she didn't speak in class anymore and complained that the professor talked only about men and what's important to them:

He, he, he is all I ever heard in that class. He wasn't speaking my language. I didn't belong . . . sometimes the boys would make jokes about girls doing science experiments. They always thought they were going to do it better and it made me really nervous. (Lewis 1990, 472–73)

Even without the overt feminist context of a classroom such as Lewis's within which Chris and Naomi might be encouraged to organize and articulate their thoughts regarding themselves and their relationship to the patriarchal culture of the schools, they have done so. It would appear that for the girls who contributed to the data described in this book, the act of participating in a girls-only grouping helped them begin to understand that they are not part of the dominant culture.

Further, being in the girls-only classes has been an affirmative experience. Here, they have been given a place where they create their own culture, where the talk is meaningful and inclusive, and where they either confirm or learn that they can "do the work."

Girls-only classes, especially those in public, coeducational schools, do not represent a mirror image of the traditional iteration of single-sex schooling. The reason for their development has not been to create a parallel educational universe for young women, but rather to create an environment that provides female students with a place to learn without experiencing the battlefield for resources.

Current research points to a host of problems faced by young women today. Eating disorders occur in early adolescent girls as they react to societal values for women (Faludi 1991). Sexual harassment in classrooms and hallways goes unreported or underreported, and even so the public statistics are alarming (Bailey 1992). Girls, much more than boys, experience what the Sadkers (1995) refer to as a self-esteem "free-fall" at the beginning of early adolescence. Within the realm of career aspiration, although their teacher-awarded grades are reported as being higher than their male counterparts in math and science classes during middle and high school, girls come to feel disenfranchised in these classes and do less well on standardized tests in these areas. Young women choose higher level math and science courses and college programs that are math and science-oriented at much lower rates than young men.

There are exceptions to these statistics to be sure. Sunny, in her second year as an engineering student, is achieving well. Her grades are high, and she enjoys the math and science courses. But still she struggles. She is suspicious of women's groups developed to mentor and support the women in engineering and worries about appearing to be different if she joins with the other women in this group. Meanwhile, she resents being isolated and treated like the perennial secretary. Despite Sunny's achievements to date, she is not unaffected by a sense of alienation and a need to fight for a place within a culture of which she is not a member.

If Sunny were to turn to Feminist and Critical theorists for advice or guidance, they would offer to her their beliefs about the underlying societal structure that creates for her this milieu of frustration and alienation. Sunny has entered the collegiate epitome of how male culture defines the essence of her experiences. According to Bordo (1990) and Downs (1993), for example, because she is of an underclass, in this case female, she cannot expect to be treated in the same ways in which European-descent males are treated.

The response of many feminists to this set of issues has been to turn to the underlying premise of Title IX, and to maintain the tenets of the early iteration of the contemporary women's movement. The best way, and perhaps the only way, to create positive change for women, is to maintain that women are the same as men. To suggest that females are different from men is to risk closing the door of access to the opportunities of the male-dominated world. Further, to suggest, as Belenky et al. (1986) would to Sunny, that because she is female, she sees the world and interprets knowledge and experiences in ways that are different from those posed through the curriculum and pedagogy in her engineering classes, is to risk the interpretation that different is less. If women are acknowledged as different from men, they will be seen as inferior, and therefore deserving of fewer opportunities and less access to places where power and prestige reside. Belenky et al. (1986) suggest that women constitute a separate culture than men—a controversial position.

In *Gender Play,* Thorne (1993) examines the construct of separate gender cultures and finds it wanting. Based on the analysis of her own ethnographic data, she suggests, for example, that when we observe classroom dynamics through the lens of gender as expressed by girls' culture and boys' culture, we create an artificial dichotomy. She maintains that the description of a boys' culture has been based on examination of too few of the boys of the entire group. One tends to focus on the "big man," or the most popular boy as well as his followers or others in his group. This over-focused view tends to disregard the affiliations and activities of other boys who do not fall into the categories that we tend to develop when describing boys—"large, public, hierarchical, competitive" (1993, 91).

In other words, there are exceptions to the generalization of how boys' culture looks. Thorne (1993) believes that our traditional description of girls' culture also oversimplifies the complex dynamics found in any group where relationships and actions are studied. Not all girls follow the rules of turn-taking or of creating small group or pair relationships.

It is hard to argue that there are individual differences operating within the larger group. Nearly any cultural definition is deficient in that it provides only the broad sweep and does not account for the behavior or beliefs of the individual. To be African American does not suggest that one is exactly like the next, but rather some general values and beliefs are held in common with others of that culture. There is commonality among the group members, as there is some difference among them. With regard to female culture, there appears to be a sufficient number of commonalties, including some serious problems, that are held in common by members of the culture (and not by others) to lead us to believe that at least to some extent, there is a women's culture.

The research conducted in Eastside Middle, Elgin High, Williams High, and Connecticut Academy resulted in findings that resonated from one classroom to the next. Whether this was a result of the fact that the girls were creating a place to work in which only their own culture was represented, or they were simply in classrooms where they could leave the dominant culture behind, one where they struggled for visibility and voice, may be a moot question. Whether or not we choose to call the girls-only classes embodying aspects of a women's culture, it appears that the young women believed that their girls-only classrooms were special places where they could take risks, be "in the front," grow as math or science students, and in general have a respite from their struggle to be heard and valued.

Girls-only classes are not a major, national phenomenon. In this study, their development was sporadic, and almost serendipitous. Teachers or principals appeared to come across the idea through various means, and then created the classes as experimental sites where they hoped students would have more opportunity to learn without distraction. The degree of commitment to the classes varied enormously. With the exception of Connecticut Academy, where commitment to girls schooling is total, principals in the public schools seemed to provide a venue of benign neglect, leaving the success of the class in the hands of the teachers.

Policy Conflicts with Reality

The record of the experiences of the girls in the single-sex classes suggests that the ethic of equality is too limiting for us to expect equal outcomes by gender as a result. In order for us to reasonably suggest that the provision of open access will assure all participants equal opportunity within the culture, we would have to assume that what is provided will benefit the groups equally. The structure, the curriculum, the materials, as well as teacher-related resources would be equally distributed and equally beneficial. We would have to assume that females and males as groups are the same, and that the culture of schools is gender neutral. These assumptions fail to hold true. The reality is that schools are places that empower boys and disenfranchise girls and the other reality is that girls are different from boys.

Whether we believe that girls and boys are different for inherent or socialization reasons, or a combination of the two, we act out that belief in our schools. We have constructed schools as places where males dominate and are more valued than girls. Under the auspices of Title IX, that is to say, the principle of equality, we provide female students equal access to an uninclusive culture. Female students must struggle to "do the work" as participants *outside* of the culture.

Girls-only classes are constructed within the principle of equity. Here, affirmative action means a place where more resources are directed toward a specific group, one where reparation is indicated. Within the patriarchal structure, to set apart a group of girls expressly for purposes of their own development and empowerment is risky. Not only do we violate the principle of equality, we risk these groups' being labelled inferior. Any group in schools, other than Euro-male, exists outside of the cultural mainstream. When integrated into that culture, the girls, in this case, have only the choice of acculturating to whatever extent they are able. What they do not have is the choice of being in a place where they begin to understand themselves, in a cultural setting in which, as Chris said, they "belong," and they "understand."

The young women who are least afforded this choice are the poor. Young women such as Kathy and Susan at Connecticut Academy, both of whom have the advantage of affluence, have the additional advantage of choice. Their families can afford to pay for the choice of a private girls-only educational setting. But the opportunities for single-sex schooling within the public domain, settings that would be accessible by the middle class and poor are few, and those are under attack.

The resistance toward the East Harlem Young Women's Leadership Academy by groups such as NOW represents an inability to acknowledge the need of poor young women to inhabit a place where they can develop themselves and their skills within a supportive and understandable culture. The school in Harlem, Girls High in Philadelphia, as well as the girls-only classrooms that exist quietly and precariously in coeducational, public schools provide a chance at equity for girls, regardless of economic class.

Final Statement

It would seem that the most fundamental issue lies between the need for authentic equitable practice and the reality brought about by Title IX. If the purpose is to treat gender inequities and perpetual disempowerment of female students on a short-term and superficial basis, then it would appear that policy and practice within the theoretical framework of equality should continue. This approach defines gender-equitable programs and practices as innovations, when they are actually quick-fix remedies that with some teacher training, can be implemented without making anyone uncomfortable.

With innovation, the balance of resource distribution is not disrupted, and the group that historically has received the greater amount of resources continues to do so.

Unfortunately, assurance of equal access to resources does not ensure equal treatment within the local classroom, nor does it create a place where beliefs and attitudes about potential and capabilities are without gender implications. Classrooms remain places where males are dominant and females are likely to feel less than equal. Too much evidence exists that tells us that an "equality" approach is not sufficiently powerful to assure equal outcomes free of gender-group disparity.

The need to realign resources, through the development of girls-only classes, must be acknowledged at the federal level. Local voices, particularly those of the girls who tell the compelling stories of their experiences in girls-only classes, must be acknowledged as legitimate. With a broader interpretation of federal policy that creates space for girls-only classes as an important direction in which gender-equity remedies might be integrated, the other actions necessary to ensure the success of these classes can be taken.

The essential training of administrators, teachers, students, and parents about gender equity in general, and in girls-only classes specifically, could become part of the culture of schools where such classes are offered. The first critical step, however, is to empower local practice through broader and more informed federal policy.

$\mathcal{A}$ppendix $\mathcal{A}$

Teacher Protocol at Connecticut Academy

Interview with Mr. Paul

1. Tell me about your background, how you came to be a teacher at CA, and about your training.

2. After your students leave the middle school setting and have some coeducational classes, have you ever talked with them about how they feel about the difference?

3. You have quite a bit of contact with CA alumni. What do the women talk about as they reflect on having gone to a girls-only school?

4. What are your beliefs about girls and science? Are these beliefs different from your beliefs about boys and science?

5. What do you believe are the benefits and drawbacks to single-sex schooling for girls?

6. All of the girls at CA are affluent. One way to introduce single-sex schooling opportunities to poor girls is to create classes in public schools, or schools like the East Harlem Young Women's Leadership Academy. Tell me what you think about these settings.

7. Describe some of the reading you have done regarding girls-only schooling, and other gender equity issues in schools.

8. Do you believe that girls have different learning styles than boys? Why?

9. Do you believe that all girls would benefit from a single-sex schooling setting?

$\mathcal{A}$ppendix $\mathcal{B}$

Teacher Protocol at Public Schools

Initial Teacher Interviews with Ms. Mary, Ms. Louise, Mr. Lincoln, Mr. Gordon, Ms. Quinn, Ms. Grace, Mr. James

1. How did you become the teacher of this girls-only class?
2. Do you have any special interest in gender-equity issues in teaching?
3. Do you have any special training in gender-equity issues in teaching?
4. Before you took over this class, did you have any opportunity to observe or learn about other girls-only classes?
5. What role has your principal had in making this class happen?
6. What do you know about any policy that affects the creation of a girls-only class in a public school?
7. How does the curriculum in this class compare to that of your other classes that are mixed-gender?
8. Do you think you teach this class any differently than you do your mixed-gender classes?
9. Do you find that boys tend to behave differently in classes than girls? Why do you think this is?
10. Do you think that there are learning style differences between boys and girls? Why?
11. Describe what it's like to have only girls in a class. Do the girls behave in ways you would have predicted? Do the girls behave differently when they are with just girls than when they are with boys?

12. Do you think this class has any effect on how well the girls learn?

13. Do you think this class has any effect on how the girls think about themselves as learners of math/science? Is there an effect on their level of confidence?

14. Do you think you behave differently in this girls-only class than you do in your other classes?

15. Do you have different discipline issues in this class than in your others?

16. Do you think having girls-only classes is a good idea? Are there some subject areas that might be more appropriate for girls-only than others?

17. If a boy wanted to enroll in this class, what do you think should happen?

18. If this class continues for more years, do you want to be the teacher?

*A*ppendix *C*

Student Protocol at Connecticut Academy

Interviews with Susan and Kathy

1. When did you start at CA?
2. Have you ever gone to a public school? A coeducational school?
3. What are some of the things you really like about being in school here? Is there anything you would like to see changed?
4. What's it like to have classes with just girls?
5. (Kathy) How are your coed classes different from your girls-only math class?
6. Why do you think CA has math as single-sex?
7. What are your favorite courses, and which ones are not your favorites?
8. (Kathy) How do you feel when you go to the boys' campus next door for classes?
9. (Susan) How do you think you'll like having classes with boys?
10. What do you want to do when you get out of high school?
11. What do your parents want you to do?
12. Tell me about how your teachers teach. Do you see a difference if the teacher is a man or a woman?
13. How do you feel about yourself as a learner of math and science?
14. What do you think are the important things to girls your age?

15. If you had it to do over again, would you want to come to this school?

16. Would you recommend this school to other girls? Why?

$\mathcal{A}$ppendix $\mathcal{D}$

Student Protocol at Public Schools

Initial Interview at Eastside Middle School with Seventh-Grade Students of Ms. Mary, Ms. Louise, Mr. Lincoln/ Mr. Gordon

1. When you first came into this class, what were your impressions?
2. What math class were you in last year?
3. Do you live in the neighborhood?
4. Have you gone to this school for all of middle school?
5. Do you have friends in this class?
6. You had the same math teacher last year. Are there things you think she does differently in a mixed-gender class than here in the girls-only class?
7. Are there differences you see in the behavior of students in the girls-only class compared to students in the mixed-gender classes?
8. What in your mind is the best thing about this class?
9. What is the worst?
10. What kind of things do boys of this age say to girls?
11. Do you think boys behave differently or the same as girls in classes?
12. If you were to change one thing about this class, what would you change?
13. Do you think the girls in this class work in ways that are different from girls and boys in other classes?

14. What do you want to do when you finish school? What are your goals? What do your parents want you to do?

15. Which subjects are your favorite subjects in school?

16. How do you think you learn math? How do you assess your own learning in this class? Is it different from other math classes you've had?

17. As a middle school girl, what kinds of things make you feel good? What are some of the things that are important to girls your age?

18. How do you feel about math? How do you feel about science? Do you think you'll want to take more math or science in high school?

19. Do you think you would like a career where you use a lot of math?

Second Interview at Eastside Middle School with Girls who had Advanced to Ms. Mary's Eighth-Grade Class

1. How would you say you feel about math now?

2. I'm interested in how you think you learn math. Are there any differences in how you learn in here with how you've learned in other math classes?

3. Are there things that your teacher does that are different from other teachers?

4. What math class do you think you'll take as a freshman in high school?

5. What do you think it will be like in a mixed-gender math class?

6. Are you feeling more, less, or about the same confidence in your math ability after having been in this class for two years?

7. Are there ways of teaching that your teacher used in here that are different from the ways your other teachers teach?

8. What do you think you want to do when you're out of school? What do your parents want you to do?

9. Do you think there are differences in the way boys and girls act in mixed-gender classes when you compare the behavior of girls in the girls-only class?

10. If there were a girls-only class in your high school, would you want to be in it? What would you want it to be?

11. Tell me how you feel about having been in this class for two years.

Third Interview with ninth-grade students, who were formerly in Ms. Mary's class at Eastside Middle School

1. What are the things you remember best about the girls-only math class?

2. Do you think the girls-only class helped prepare you better, the same, or not as well for your current math class than if you'd been in a mixed-gender math class?

3. What math class are you taking now? What's it like? Is math hard, easy, or somewhere in between this year? Why do you think it's that way? Was there anything from the girls-only class that is making math easier, harder, or the same this year?

4. What are the differences in having boys in your math class now and not having had them in your class at Eastside?

5. Do you have a man or woman for your teacher? What is that like? Would you rather have (the other gender) for your teacher? Why?

6. Do you think it was important to have a woman for your girls-only math class? Why?

7. Do you have any friends in your math class? Any from last year? Does that make a difference to you?

8. If there were a girls-only math class for the math you are currently taking, would you take that class? Why?

9. Are there any other girls-only classes you wish you could take?

10. Would you recommend the girls-only math class at Eastside Middle to seventh- and eighth-grade girls? Why?

11. Will you take a math class next year? Why, and if yes, which one?

12. How did you feel about math last year? How do you feel about math now?

13. When you have a problem in math, do you feel you can ask the teacher for help during class? Do you ask for help after class?

14. Does the teacher seem to call on either girls or boys more often than the other gender? Why do you think that is?

15. Do you talk in your math class now? Do you raise your hand to answer questions in class? Why or why not?

16. In your math class, do the people work alone mostly, or does the teacher have people work in groups? Do you like that? Why?

17. When you don't understand the homework for math, how do you figure it out? Do you ask someone for help?

18. Is there someone in your home who you go to, to help you with your math if you have a problem? Why that person?

19. Do you plan on going to college? If yes, do you think you will take any math classes in college?

20. What do you think you want to do when you are finished with school?

Initial Interview (Fall Semester) with Students in All-Girls Physics Class at Elgin High School

1. Why did you decide to take this class?

2. Do you find yourself feeling any differently about science than you have in other science classes you've had?

3. Do you feel any different about studying science in this class than in others you've had?

4. Do you have any sense of how this class may shape how you feel about science?

5. Tell me a little bit about science classes you've taken before.

6. What do you like about this class so far?

7. Do you think anything should be changed about the class?

8. Do you have friends from other classes in this class?

9. Does the behavior of boys in classes make a difference to you?

10. Tell me about your career goals.

11. What do your parents want you to do when you finish high school?

12. Would you recommend a girls-only class to other girls?

13. What do you think is important to girls your age?

Second Interview (Spring Semester) with Students in
All-Girls Physics Class at Elgin High School

1. Now that you've been in this class for nearly a year, tell me about the differences you see in this class compared to other science classes you've had.

2. Tell me about whether you think the teacher in this class teaches differently in this class than teachers in mixed-gender classes.

3. What's it like being in a class without boys?

4. What's it like being in a class with only girls?

5. Do you have any feelings about science now that might be different than if you hadn't been in this class.

6. Do you hear anything about this girls-only class from people in this school who aren't in this class?

7. What do you want to do after high school?

8. If you plan on going to college, what do you think you'll major in?

9. Do you think you'll take any science classes in college?

10. Would you recommend this class to other girls at Elgin? Why or why not?

11. What do you think is important to girls your age?

Third Interview with Students Who Were Formerly in All-Girls Physics Class at Elgin High School and at the Time of This Interview are at the End of Their Freshman Year in College

1. What have you been doing this past school year?

2. What will you do this next school year?

3. How have you liked your first year in college?

4. What courses have you taken in college, and what will you take this next year?

5. How have these classes gone for you? (Focus on math and science classes.)

6. What would you name as your most difficult class last year? Why?

7. When you started this last year, what did you think your major was going to be and is it the same at the end of the year as it was at the beginning?

8. When you look back on your experiences in the girls-only physics class, what do you remember about it that was good?

9. And can you think of anything, at this point, that might have not been so good?

10. When you look back do you think that any aspect of that class made a difference in any way or any impact on you this year?

11. Do you think there was any effect, one way or the other, with regard to your confidence in taking science in college?

12. Did you notice anything in your classes that you took this year that you would consider to be a gender issue? For example, the number of males vs. females in the classes, any gender-related issues in how people behave in classes?

13. What about the gender of your instructors this year? Do you think that makes any difference?

14. How was your science class structured this year? Was it different from the girls-only physics class, or similar?

15. In your classes now, do you work on your own, or is there group work, or are they mostly large lecture?

16. Did you feel uncomfortable in any of your classes this year for any reason? How?

17. If you had the chance to take a female-only class now, would you? If so, what would it be and why?

18. If you could make any changes in your classes this past year, based on your girls-only physics class experience, what might the changes be?

19. If you could go back to the girls at Elgin, what would you tell them about your girls-only experience, and about your experiences this past year in college?

20. Would you recommend a girls-only physics, or any other subject matter, class to girls in high school?

Initial Interview (Fall Semester) at Williams High School with Girls in Foundations Math Class

1. How did you come to be in this class?

2. Do you feel any differently about math, compared to how you used to feel in your other math classes?

3. Do you think that being in this girls-only math class might make a difference in how you feel about math?

4. Tell me about other math classes you took before you took this one.

5. Do you think boys behave differently in classes than girls? Does that make a difference to you?

6. Do you think girls behave differently in this class than they do in other classes? Are you different in here than in other classes?

7. Do you think your teachers in this class teach differently than they would in mixed-gender classes?

8. Can you think of anything you'd like to see changed in this class?

9. What do you like, and what don't you like about it?

10. Do you have friends in this class? Does that make a difference to you?

11. What do you want to do after high school?

12. What do your parents want you to do?

13. What do you think is important to girls your age?

14. At this point, would you recommend this class to other girls at Williams, or to younger girls who will come to this school?

Second Interview (Spring Semester) at Williams High School with Girls in Foundations Math Class

1. Now that you've been in this class almost a year, how do you feel about having been in a girls-only math class?

2. Do you think you feel any differently about math now than you did before you were in this class?

3. What has it been like being in a class without boys?

4. What has it been like being in a class with just girls?

5. Do you think your teachers have taught this class differently from other classes you have?

6. Do you think your teachers have taught this class differently from other classes they teach?

7. What would you change about this class for the next time?

8. What have been the good things about this class?

9. What do you want to do after high school?

10. What things are important to girls your age?

11. If you could take another girls-only class, would you do that? If yes, what would you want the subject to be?

12. Would you recommend this class to other girls?

References

Arends, R. I. 1988. *Learning to teach.* New York: Random House.

Arnot, M. 1982. Male hegemony, social class, and women's education. In *The education feminism reader,* ed. L. Stone, 84–104. New York: Routledge.

Astin, W. A. 1977. *Four critical years: Effects of college and beliefs, attitudes and knowledge.* San Francisco: Jossey-Bass.

Bailey, S. M. 1992. *The AAUW report: How schools shortchange girls.* Wellesley: Wellesley College, Center for Research on Women.

Banks, T. L. 1988. Gender bias in the classroom. *Journal of Legal Education* 38 (1–2): 137–146.

Belenky, M. F., B. M. Clinchy, N. R. Goldberg, and J. M. Tarule. 1986. *Women's ways of knowing: The development of self, voice, and mind.* New York: Basic Books.

Bell, J. 1989. A comparison of science performance and uptake by fifteen-year-old girls in co-educational and single-sex schools—APU Survey findings. *Educational Studies* 15: 193–203.

Bordo, S. 1990. Feminism, postmodernism, and gender-skepticism. In *Feminism / postmodernism,* ed. L. Nicholson, 133–156. New York: Routledge.

Bowles, S., and H. Gintis. 1976. *Schooling in capitalist America: Educational reform and the contradictions of economic life.* New York: Basic Books.

Cairns, E. 1990. The relationship between adolescent perceived self-competence and attendance at single-sex secondary school. *British Journal of Educational Psychology* 60: 207–211.

Carpenter, P., and M. Hayden. July 1987. Girls' academic achievements: Single sex versus coeducational schools in Australia. *Sociology of Education* 60.

Charricoates, K. 1980. The importance of being earnest . . . Emma . . . Tom . . . Jane. The perception and categorization of gender conformity and gender deviation in primary schools. In *Schooling for women's work,* ed. R. Deem, 26–41. London and Boston: Routledge and Kegan Paul.

Clabaugh, G. K., and E. G. Razycki. 1990. *Understanding schools: The foundations of education.* New York: Harper & Row.

Coleman, J. 1961. *The adolescent society.* New York: Free Press of Glencoe.

Digest of Education Statistics. 1996. National Center for Education Statistics, U. S. Department of Education, Office of Research and Improvement.

Donovan, J. 1985. *Feminist theory: The intellectual traditions of American feminism.* New York: Frederick Ungar.

Downs, L. L. 1993. If "woman" is just an empty category, then why am I afraid to walk alone at night? Identity politics meets postmodern subject. *Comparative Studies in Society and History* 35: 414–437.

Ebbeck, M. 1984. Equity for boys and girls: Some important issues. *Early Child Development and Care* 18: 119–131.

Excerpts from high court's ruling against the male-only policy of V. M. I. (27 June 1996). *The New York Times,* C18.

Faludi, S. 1991. *Backlash: The undeclared war against American women.* New York: Crown Publishers, Inc.

Fennema, E., and P. Peterson. 1987. Effective teaching for girls and boys: The same or different? In *Talks to teachers,* eds. D. Berliner and B. Rosenshine Eds., 111–125. New York: Random House.

Fox, L. H., L. Brody, and D. Tobin. 1980. *Women and the mathematical mystiques.* Baltimore: Johns Hopkins University Press.

Freire, P. 1993. *Pedagogy of the oppressed.* New York: Continuum.

Giroux, H. A. 1983. Theories of reproduction and resistance in the new sociology of education: A critical analysis. *Harvard Educational Review* 53 (3): 257–293.

Gore, J. M. 1993. *The struggle for pedagogies: Critical and feminist discourses as regimes of truth.* New York: Routledge.

Grayson, D. A., and M. D. Martin. 1985. *Gender expectations and student achievement.* Los Angeles County Office of Education, Division of Project Funding and Management.

Greene, K. R. 1992. Models of school board policy-making. *Educational Administrator Quarterly* 28 (2): 220–236.

Guinier, L. 1994. Becoming gentlemen: Women's experiences at one Ivy League law school. *University of Pennsylvania Law Review* 143: 1–110.

Hamilton, M. A. 1985. Performance levels in science and other subjects for Jamaican adolescents attending single-sex and co-educational high schools. *International Science Education* 69 (4): 535–547.

Harvey, T. J. November 1985. Science in single-sex and mixed teaching groups. *Educational Research* 27 (3): 179–182.

Hollinger, D., ed. 1993. *Single-sex schooling: Perspectives from practice and research.* A special report from the Office of Educational Research and Improvement, U. S. Department of Education Vol. 1.

Hollinger, D. K., and R. Adamson, eds. 1993. *Single-sex schooling: Proponents speak.* A special report from the Office of Educational Research and Improvement, U. S. Department of Education Vol. II.

hooks, b. 1993. Bell Hooks speaking about Paulo Freire—the man, his works. In *Paulo Freire: A critical encounter,* eds. P. McLaren and P. Leonard, 146–154. London and New York: Routledge.

IMSA. 1995. *Statement: 1993–94 calculus-based physics/mechanics study.* Illinois Mathematics and Science Academy, 1500 W. Sullivan Road, Aurora, IL 60506-1000.

Irvine, J. J. 1986. Teacher–student interactions: Effects of student race, sex, and grade level. *Journal of Educational Psychology* 78 (1): 14–21.

Jacklin, P. 1981. The concept of sex equity in jurisprudence. In *Educational policy and management: Sex differentials,* eds. P. A. Chaters Jr. and R. O. Carlson. New York: Academic Press.

Johnson, D. W., and R. T. Johnson. 1975. *Learning together and alone: Cooperation, competition, and individualization.* Englewood Cliffs, N.J.: Prentice-Hall.

Johnson, D. W., and R. T. Johnson. 1994. *Learning together and alone: Cooperative, competitive, and individualistic learning* (4th ed.). Needham Heights, Mass.: Allyn and Bacon.

Lather, P. 1988. Feminist perspectives on emancipatory research methodologies. *Women's Studies International Forum* 11: 569–581.

Lee, V. E., and A. Bryk. 1986. Effects of single secondary schools on student achievement and attitudes. *Journal of Educational Psychology* 78: 381–395.

Lee, V. E., R. G. Croninger, E. Linn, and X. Chen. Summer 1996. The culture of sexual harassment in secondary schools. *American Educational Research Journal* 33 (2): 383–417.

Lee, V. E., and H. M. Marks. 1990. Sustained effects of the single-sex secondary school experience on attitudes, behaviors, and values in college. *Journal of Educational Psychology* 82 (3): 578–592.

Lee, V. E., and H. M. Marks. 1992. Who goes where? Choice of single-sex and coeducational independent secondary schools. *Sociology in Education* 65: 226–253.

Lee, V. E., H. M. Marks, and T. Byrd. 1994. Sexism in single-sex and coeducational independent secondary school classrooms. *Sociology of Education* 67 April: 92–120.

LePore, P. C., and J. R. Warren. 1997. A comparison of single-sex and coeducational Catholic secondary schooling: Evidence from the National Educational Longitudinal Study of 1988. *American Educational Research Journal* 34 (3): 485–511.

Lewis, M. 1990. Interrupting patriarchy: Politics, resistance, and transformation in the feminist classroom. *Harvard Educational Review* 60 (4): 467–486.

Lindsey, L. 1997. *Gender roles: A sociological perspective.* Upper Saddle River, N.J.: Prentice Hall.

Mann, J. 1996. *The Difference.* New York: Warner Books.

Marsh, H. W. 1989a. Effects of attending single-sex and coeducational high schools on achievement, attitudes, behaviors, and sex differences. *Journal of Educational Psychology* 81 (1): 70–85.

———. 1989b. Effects of single-sex and coeducational schools: A response to Lee and Bryk. *Journal of Educational Psychology* 81 (4): 651–653.

McLaren, P., and P. Leonard, eds., 1993. *Paulo Freire: A critical encounter.* London & New York: Routledge.

Meyer, W. J., and G. G. Thompson. 1956. Sex differences in the distribution of teacher approval and disapproval among sixth-grade children. *Journal of Educational Psychology* 27: 385–397.

Moll, L. 1994. Literacy research in community and classrooms. In *Theoretical models and processes of reading,* eds. R. B. Ruddell, M. R. Ruddell, and H. Singer (4th ed.). Newark, Del.: International Reading Association.

National Coalition of Girls' Schools. 1995. *Choosing a Girls' School.*

Nicholson, L. J. 1980. Women and schooling. In *The education feminism reader,* ed. L. Stone, 73–83. New York: Routledge.

Orenstein, P. 1994. *SchoolGirls: Young women, self-esteem and the confidence gap.* New York: Doubleday.

Pierson, R. R. 1987. Two Marys and a Virginia: Historical moments in the development of a feminist perspective on education. In *Women and education: A Canadian perspective,* eds. J. Gaskell and A. McLaren, 203–222. Calgary: Detselig Enterprises.

Pipher, M., 1994. *Reviving Ophelia.* New York: Ballantine Books.

Rice, J. K., and A. Hemmings. 1988. Women's colleges and women achievers: An update. *Journal of Educational Psychology* 47: 385–397.

Riordan, C. August 1985. Public and Catholic schooling: The effects of gender context policy. *American Journal of Education*: 518–540.

———. 1990. *Girls and boys in school: Together or separate?* New York: Teachers College Press.

Rowe, K. J. 1988. Single-sex and mixed-sex classes: The effects of class type on student achievement, confidence and participation in mathematics. *Australian Journal of Education* 32: 180–202.

Sadker, M., and D. Sadker. 1982. *Sex equity handbook for schools.* New York: McGraw-Hill.

Sadker, M., and D. Sadker. 1995. *Failing at fairness: How our schools cheat girls.* New York: Touchstone.

Sanchez, R. (29 June 1996). Citadel parts with past, opens ranks to women; court ruling forces all-male college's hand. *The Washington Post,* p. A3.

Sherman, J. 1980. Mathematics, spatial visualization, and related factors: Changes in girls and boys, grades 8–11. *Journal of Educational Psychology* 72: 476–482.

Shor, I. 1980. *Critical teaching and everyday life.* Boston: South End Press.

Slavin, R. 1983. *Cooperative learning.* New York: Longman.

Slavin, R. E. 1995. *Cooperative learning: Theory, research, and practice* (2nd ed.). Boston: Allyn and Bacon.

Smith, D. G. 1990. Women's colleges and coed colleges: Is there a difference for women? *Journal of Higher Education* 61 (2): 181–197.

Spender, D. 1982. *Invisible women: The schooling scandal.* London: Writers and Readers.

Steedman, J. 1985. Examination results in mixed and single-sex secondary schools. In *Studying school effectiveness,* ed. D. Reynolds, 87–101. London: The Falmer Press.

Steinberg, J. (16 July 1996). Plans for Harlem girls school faces concern over sex bias. *The New York Times,* A1.

Steinberg, J. (14 August 1996). All-Girls' public school is set for Harlem despite objections. *The New York Times,* A16.

Stock, P. 1978. *Better than rubies: A history of women's education.* New York: G. P. Putnam's Sons.

Stone, L., ed. 1994. *The education feminism reader.* New York: Routledge.

Streitmatter, J. 1994. *Toward gender equity in the classroom: Everyday teachers' beliefs and practices.* Albany: SUNY Press.

Stromquist, N. 1993. Sex equity legislation in education: The state as promoter of women's rights. *Review of Educational Research* 63 (4): 379–407.

Tabor, M. B. W. (22 July 1996). Planners of new public school for girls are studying two other cities. *The New York Times.*

Thorne, B. 1993. *Gender play: Girls and boys in school.* New Brunswick, N.J.: Rutgers University Press.

Tidball, M. E. 1973. Perspective on academic women and affirmative action. *Educational Record* 54: 130–135.

———. 1980. Women's colleges and women achievers revisited. *Signs: Journal of Women in Culture and Society* 5: 504–517.

———. 1985. Baccalaureate origins of entrants into American medical schools. *Journal of Higher Education* 56: 385–402.

———. 1986. Baccalaureate origins of recent natural science doctorates. *Journal of Higher Education* 57: 606–620.

Trickett, E. J., P. K. Trickett, J. J. Castro, and P. Schaffr.er. 1982. The independent school experience: Aspects of the normative environments of single-sex and coed secondary schools. *Journal of Educational Psychology* 74 (3): 374–381.

Tyack, D., and E. Hansot. 1990. *Learning together: A history of coeducation in American schools.* New Haven and London: Yale University Press.

U. S. Department of Education. 1996. Office of Educational Research and Improvement, Washington, D.C.

U. S. General Accounting Office. May 1996. *Public education: Issues involving single-gender schools and programs.* Report to the Chairman, Committee on the Budget, House of Representatives. GAO/HEHS-96–122.

Vorchheimer v. School District of Philadelphia. 1976. 532 F.2d 880 3d Cir. 1976, affirmed by an equally divided court, 430 U.S. 703 1977.

Weitzman, L., and D. Rizzo. 1976. *Biased textbooks and images of males and females in elementary school textbooks.* Washington, D.C.: Resource Center on Sex Roles in Education.

Women on Words and Images. 1975. *Dick and Jane as victims: Sex stereotyping in children's readers, help wanted: Sexism in career educational materials.* Princeton: Princeton University Press.

Index